C000090821

THE LONDON, MIDLAND SCOTTISH RAILWAY

—— VOLUME FOUR ——

MANCHESTER TO LEEDS

Stanley C. Jenkins & Martin Loader

AMBERLEY

ACKNOWLEDGEMENTS

Most of the photographs used in this publication were obtained from the Lens of Sutton Collection and from the authors' own collections. Thanks are due to Roger Sutcliffe for the supply of additional colour photographs of Manchester Victoria and Miles Platting stations.

A Note on Closure Dates

British Railways closure announcements referred to the first day upon which services would no longer run, which would normally have been a Monday. However, the final day of operation would usually have been the preceding Sunday (or, if there was no Sunday service, the preceding Saturday). In other words, closure would take place on a Saturday or Sunday, whereas the 'official' closure would become effective with effect from the following Monday.

A recent photograph of the Grade II-listed station building at Mytholmroyd, which is out of use at the time of writing.

First published 2016

Amberley Publishing
The Hill, Stroud, Gloucestershire, GL5 4EP
www.amberley-books.com

Copyright © Stanley C. Jenkins & Martin Loader, 2016

The right of Stanley C. Jenkins & Martin Loader to be identified as the Authors of this work has been asserted in accordance with the Copyrights, Designs and Patents Act 1988.

ISBN 978 1 4456 4388 5 (print)
ISBN 978 1 4456 4414 1 (ebook)

All rights reserved. No part of this book may be reprinted or reproduced or utilised in any form or by any electronic, mechanical or other means, now known or hereafter invented, including photocopying and recording, or in any information storage or retrieval system, without the permission in writing from the Publishers.

British Library Cataloguing in Publication Data.
A catalogue record for this book is available from the British Library.

Printed in Great Britain.

INTRODUCTION

The availability of cheap and efficient transport was an important factor in the Industrial Revolution and, by the early nineteenth century, manufacturing towns such as Rochdale, Oldham and Burnley were able to benefit from the provision of turnpike road links to Manchester, Preston, and other destinations. The industrial towns of East Lancashire were also linked by the Leeds & Liverpool Canal, which had been authorised by an Act of Parliament in 1770. Sections of the waterway were open at each end by 1777, but financial problems and engineering difficulties meant that this ambitious 127-mile waterway was not fully completed until 1816.

Meanwhile, on 4 April 1794, the promoters of the Rochdale Canal had obtained parliamentary consent for a waterway link across the Pennines from Manchester to a junction with the Calder & Hebble Navigation at Sowerby Bridge; this broad gauge waterway reached Rochdale in 1799. These trans-Pennine waterways were an immense advantage to local traders and industrialists but, with the rapid development of rail transport during the 1830s and 1840s, it became clear that towns such as Rochdale, Oldham, Burnley and Todmorden needed a rail link to the outside world.

ORIGINS OF THE MANCHESTER & LEEDS RAILWAY

Plans for a railway across the Pennines from Manchester to Leeds were under discussion as early as the 1820s, although nothing positive was achieved until the following decade, when an undertaking known as 'The Manchester & Leeds Railway' was formed to construct the hoped-for trans-Pennine link. The scheme was sanctioned by Parliament on 4 July 1836, and the promoters were thereby empowered to construct a railway commencing at Manchester and terminating at Normanton, from where the M&LR would have running powers into Leeds over the North Midland Railway.

Although Leeds was only 35 miles from Manchester, the hilly nature of the surrounding countryside meant that George Stephenson, the company's chief engineer, was obliged to adopt a circuitous route. The authorised line climbed to a height of 545 feet above mean sea level as it meandered first north, then eastwards, through Rochdale and Todmorden to Hebden Bridge. Beyond, the chosen route followed the sinuous and steep-sided Calder Valley towards Eland, from where the river's floodplain provided an easier path through Brighouse and Rastrick to Goose Hill Junction, where the proposed line converged with the North Midland Railway. The total distance from Manchester to Leeds via Rochdale, Todmorden and the Calder Valley would be 60 miles 56 chains.

The first sod was ceremonially cut on 18 August 1837, the intention being that the line would be opened in the first instance between Manchester and Rochdale. The first contract, for construction of a 68-arch viaduct in Manchester, was let to John Brogden (1798–1869) in September, while further contracts were awarded to various other contractors, including Messrs Tredwells & Gerard, and Messrs James & George Thornton – the contractors being subject to heavy penalties if they did not complete the line to Rochdale by May 1839.

An interesting feature of the Manchester & Leeds Railway scheme was the involvement of Thomas Longridge Gooch (1808–82), the eldest brother of the future GWR chairman, who had been apprenticed to George Stephenson in 1823. Following the authorisation of the Manchester & Leeds line, Gooch was nominated as the 'Joint

Principal Engineer', in conjunction with George Stephenson. Daniel Gooch also became involved with the M&LR and, having written to his brother to ask if any work was available, he went to Rochdale on 25 May 1837 and began work on the M&LR. Sir Daniel later recalled that 'we were a large party living together at the Roebuck Inn at Rochdale and had some good fun. It was a pleasant time and I obtained some useful experience in levelling and surveying etc in connexion with the laying out of a railway'.

The Manchester to Rochdale portion was well advanced by the summer of 1838 and, on 14 September 1838, *The Times* reported that contracts been let for 'all the heavy works on the line', and in most cases 'very considerable progress' had been made. Between 3,000 and 4,000 navvies were at work along the southern section of the line between Manchester and Littleborough, and there was every indication that the railway would be completed throughout in 1840. In the course of a detailed report, the paper added that the Manchester terminus of the line would be in Lees Street (St George's Road), near its junction with Oldham Road. With a length of 1 mile and 1,125 yards, the Summit Tunnel between Littleborough and Walsden would obviously 'be the heaviest piece of work on the whole line', while the largest embankment would occur 'were the line crossed the River Irk near a place called Mills Hill', around three quarters of a mile to the east of Middleton.

The first section of the Manchester & Leeds Railway route was ready for opening between Manchester (Oldham Road) and Littleborough on Wednesday 3 July 1839, the great day being marked in appropriate fashion by the running of special trains for the directors, shareholders and their invited VIP guests – some 400 people in all. The opening-day celebrations were described in meticulous detail by the *Leeds Mercury*, which, on Saturday 6 July, reported that two inaugural trains were provided, 'each of great length and crowded with passengers'. Two engines were placed at the head of each train, the *Stephenson* and the *Kenyon* (both of which had been built by Messrs R. Stephenson & Co.) drew the first train, while the *Stanley* (made by Messrs Stephenson) and the *Lancaster* (made by Messrs Sharp Roberts & Co.) drew the second train. These 'new locomotive engines, shining in polished brass and steel', were said to resemble 'in size and gorgeous appearance the elephants of an eastern pageant, though very different in their speed'.

The first train consisted of five first-class carriages, three second-class carriages, and three third-class carriages, the coaches being adorned in a bright-yellow colour scheme which presented 'a very lively effect'. The first-class carriages resembled those on the Liverpool & Manchester Railway in comfort and appearance, while the second-class carriages were like the first class in dimensions and 'quite covered in', but without linings, cushions or carpets. They were partly open at the sides and had no windows, whereas the third-class vehicles were merely open trucks without seats, affording only standing room.

The first train left Manchester at 12.22 p.m., with George Stephenson riding in the guard's position on top of the first carriage, while Thomas Gooch was aboard the second locomotive. The second 'First Day Special' departed around ten minutes later; both trains then proceeded in triumph through cuttings and along embankments – the 'great Newton excavation' being 2 miles long, while the embankment beside 'Mr Becker's vitriol works' was around 50 feet high. Mills Hill station was reached in seventeen minutes, but having travelled approximately 7 miles from Manchester, it became apparent that the leading train was slowing down, as the driver of the *Kenyon* had allowed the water in the boiler to get so low that the fusible plug had melted and the remaining water had put out the fire. Undeterred by this incident, Stephenson and Gooch waited for the second train to arrive, and the two trains then resumed their journey towards Rochdale as a single working hauled by four engines.

'From the next embankment', continued the *Leeds Mercury*, a series of beautiful views 'were obtained of the blue hills and moors of north Lancashire, forming a fine background to the rapidly changing views in the valley of the Roch'. Passing by Castleton Hall, the property of John Entwhistle Esq of Foxholes, the train soon reached Rochdale, where it drew up amid cheers of the inhabitants. The station and was 'very gaily decorated' with handsome flags, and a flag also floated over the ancient church. The station, 'a spacious and commodious building', was nearly completed, and a little beyond was 'a locomotive engine house, built after a neat design'. The railway entered the town upon a viaduct, crossing the canal and the Oldham and Rochdale turnpike road 'by beautiful iron arches constructed by Messrs Newton & Galloway of Manchester'.

The crippled *Kenyon* having been detached and shunted into a siding at Rochdale, the inaugural special continued north-eastwards to Littleborough, where 'a very handsome cold collation' had been provided by Mr King, of the Bush Inn. After the usual speeches and toasts had been made, the two trains returned to Manchester. Regular public services commenced on Thursday 4 July 1839, with a daily service of seven trains each way between Manchester and the temporary terminus at Littleborough, from where coaches provided connecting road services to Leeds and Bradford. The only intermediate stations provided between Manchester and Littleborough at the time of opening were at Rochdale and Mills Hill, although other stopping places subsequently appeared, including Castleton (between Manchester and Rochdale) on 15 September 1839, and Walsden (between Rochdale and Littleborough) in October 1845).

Further sections were opened on 5 October 1840 and 3 January 1841, and the Manchester & Leeds line was opened throughout between Manchester and Normanton on 1 March 1841. The completed railway was heavily engineered, the Summit Tunnel between Littleborough and Walsden being the longest in the world at the time of its construction. A contemporary account described the 'air of Alpine grandeur' which characterised this trans-Pennine route, while a special coach known as 'The Tourist' enabled passengers to admire the passing scenery.

FORMATION OF THE LANCASHIRE & YORKSHIRE RAILWAY

On 15 April 1841, the Manchester & Leeds Railway opened a short branch from Castleton to Heywood and, in 1845, powers were obtained for a 4-mile westwards extension from Heywood to Bury. At the same time, an undertaking known as 'The Liverpool & Bury Railway' was incorporated, with powers for the construction of a line between Liverpool, Wigan, Bolton and Bury. This company was intimately connected with the Manchester & Leeds Railway and the two were ultimately amalgamated on 18 August 1846. In the following year, the enlarged company changed its name to 'The Lancashire & Yorkshire Railway' (L&YR) under the provisions of an Act of Parliament obtained on 9 July 1847.

The Heywood to Bury line was opened to Bury Knowsley Street on 1 May 1848, and the connecting line from Liverpool, Wigan and Bolton was completed on 20 November 1848. The Liverpool, Wigan and Bolton section became an integral part of the Lancashire & Yorkshire main line from Manchester to Liverpool, whereas the Bolton, Bury and Rochdale section developed into an important cross-country link for trans-Pennine traffic.

The Manchester & Leeds line passed around 3 miles to the west of Oldham but, on 31 March 1842, a line was opened from a new station known as 'Oldham Junction' to Oldham (Werneth). Oldham Junction station, which replaced nearby Mills Hill, was renamed 'Middleton Junction' in August 1842 and 'Middleton' in May 1852. On 1 November 1847, the branch line was extended eastwards from Werneth to Oldham Central and Oldham Mumps. The Oldham branch incorporated a 1 in 27 rope-worked incline at Werneth – a stationary engine being used until 1851, after which the fearsome three-quarter-mile incline was worked entirely by locomotives.

In the next few years, the Lancashire & Yorkshire Railway was able to consolidate its position in the Oldham and Rochdale area. For example, on 2 November 1863, a northwards extension was opened between Oldham (Mumps) and the original Manchester & Leeds Railway route at Rochdale. This new line formed the northern section of a circuitous loop from Middleton Junction, through Oldham, to Rochdale.

At its northern end, the Oldham Loop joined the L&YR main line by a junction that faced towards Manchester so that trains could follow an out-and-back route via Manchester and Oldham. However, operational problems posed by the notorious 1 in 27 Werneth incline were an impediment to the development of traffic and it was, in consequence, decided that a more direct line would be constructed between Manchester and Oldham. This new line, which was opened on 17 April 1880 and ran via Hollinwood and Failsworth, joined the original Manchester & Leeds route at Newton Heath. It soon became established as the principal route between Oldham and Manchester, although the original branch line from Middleton Junction was not entirely superseded and it remained in use for local traffic.

EXPANSION OF THE SYSTEM

Various other lines were promoted during the period of hectic speculation known as 'The Railway Mania', one of these new routes being the 'Copy Pit' line, which extended westwards from Todmorden to Burnley and was opened by the L&YR on Monday 12 November 1849. *The Blackburn Standard* reported that the first train 'started at a quarter to seven in the morning, and of course a numerous assemblage of spectators were assembled to witness the opening of another highway to the now busy and thriving town of Burnley'. The paper added that there were three intermediate stations on the line between Todmorden and Burnley, these being at Portsmouth, Holmes Chapel and a place called Organ Row. Curiously, the writer of the newspaper report hoped that the railway company could be prevailed upon to change the name of the latter station to Burnley Wood, as 'not one in a hundred' people knew where Organ Row was! In the event, the name of the station was subsequently changed to Towneley.

When first opened in 1849, the line from Todmorden had terminated in a small station at Burnley known as 'Thorneybank', but this was replaced by an improved station on the opposite side of Manchester Road, which was opened on 1 November 1866. The Copy Pit line continued westwards from its original terminus at Burnley to Gannow Junction, at which point it joined the East Lancashire route from Preston and, as such, it became part of a much longer cross-country route from Leeds to Blackpool.

In 1845, a company known as The West Riding Union Railways was formed as a combination of the West Yorkshire Railway and the Leeds & West Riding Junction Railways. The scheme was sanctioned by Parliament in August 1845, and the WRU promoters were thereby empowered to construct a system of lines, including a main line linking Leeds, Bradford and Halifax, the Bailiff Bridge branch from Pickle Bridge (Wyke) to Brighouse, the Low Moor to Mirfield branch, and a direct line between Halifax and Huddersfield.

The WRU Act stipulated that the West Riding Union Railway should be merged with the Manchester & Leeds Railway three months after the passing of the Act. This was duly carried out but, having obtained Parliamentary consent for an extension to Leeds and other important lines, the L&YR (as successor to the Manchester & Leeds Co.) showed little interest in the West Riding Union lines, and only a fraction of the proposed WRU system was ever constructed. However, on 1 July 1844, the L&YR had opened a branch from

Greetland to Halifax and, on 9 May 1850, the company opened the WRU route from Low Moor to Bradford. This was followed, on 7 August 1850, by the opening of the WRU line between Halifax and Low Moor; these three lines furnished the L&YR with a through route to Bradford that has remained in use until the present day.

Another line promoted at this time was a short branch from Rochdale to Bacup. This 9-mile line had an extremely long gestation period, insofar as parliamentary consent for a branch from Rochdale to Bacup had been obtained by the Manchester & Leeds Railway as long ago as 1846, but the powers were allowed to lapse and nothing further was done until 1862, when the Lancashire & Yorkshire Railway obtained new powers for a branch along the Spodden Valley to Facit.

In engineering terms, the authorised route was by no means an easy proposition: the works included a major viaduct across the River Roch at Rochdale and a further viaduct over the Spodden. Despite these difficulties, the railway builders made excellent progress and the line was opened on 1 November 1870. Eleven years later, on 1 December 1881, the branch was extended north and westwards to Bacup, where connection was made with the East Lancashire branch from Rawtenstall, which had been opened on 1 October 1852. The completed Rochdale to Bacup line was characterised by some steep gradients, as Bacup and Rochdale are sited on different sides of a ridge of much higher land, necessitating a climb of 1 in 39 to Britannia summit and a descent of 1 in 34 into Bacup.

A further line appeared in the 1870s when the North Lancashire Loop line was constructed from Great Harwood Junction, near Blackburn, to Rose Grove, near Burnley. This 9-mile line was opened from Rose Grove to Padiham on 1 September 1876, and completed throughout to Great Harwood Junction on Monday 15 October 1877. The final cost was around £300,000, making the North Lancashire Loop the most expensive line ever constructed by the L&YR. The line generated a certain amount of local passenger traffic, but it was more important as a freight-carrying route, insofar as it served a number of cotton mills, coal mines and other lineside industries.

THE SYSTEM IN OPERATION

The rail system between Manchester and Leeds formed part of a complex web of interconnecting branch lines and secondary routes. In general, the Lancashire & Yorkshire Railway network had no great trunk routes, and in this way the railway was not a main line in the sense that the Midland or North Western railways were main lines. There were, it is true, certain longer-distance L&YR services for which the company provided some very fine locomotives and rolling stock, but these services invariably worked through to York, Newcastle or other destinations over other companies' lines. There were, on the other hand, several distinct L&YR routes, among them the Manchester and Leeds line (also known as The Calder Valley route) and the busy line between Liverpool and Manchester, which were undeniably of main line character – although the distances involved were relatively modest.

In pre-Grouping days, there was a basic 'hourly interval' train service between Manchester Victoria, Leeds and Bradford, many of the eastbound workings being timed to depart from Manchester at 25 minutes past the hour. Trains generally called at Rochdale, Todmorden, Hebden Bridge and Sowerby Bridge, while many services were divided into separate Leeds and Bradford portions at Halifax or Low Moor. Halifax was served by all trains, but Rochdale and the other intermediate stations were normally served on an alternate basis. The usual journey times were 75 minutes for the 40½ miles between Manchester Victoria and Bradford Exchange, and 80 minutes for the 48¾ miles between Manchester and Leeds Central (using the GNR route between Laisterdyke and Leeds).

Many of these workings were in fact through workings to and from Liverpool Exchange. In the westbound direction, the best train was the 10.15 a.m. from Leeds, which reached Manchester in 73 minutes, with two intermediate stops.

Cecil J. Allen recalled that most trains were composed of three-coach non-corridor sets weighing no more than 80 tons gross, which ran between Leeds and Liverpool, and three-coach Bradford sets, which were attached to the Liverpool portions between Manchester and Low Moor. Some trains, however, were formed of somewhat heavier corridor stock, notably the morning and evening Liverpool to Newcastle through trains and the 'Fleetwood Boat Train', which also worked a midday round trip from Leeds to Liverpool. At the southern end of the line, there was a reasonably good service of stopping trains via the Oldham loop, and this line was also served by through carriages between Rochdale, Oldham and London Euston.

On 1 January 1922, the Lancashire & Yorkshire Railway was amalgamated with the London & North Western Railway, while in 1923 the enlarged L&NWR was itself amalgamated with the Midland and other west coast companies to form the London Midland & Scottish Railway. The Grouping inevitably brought rationalisation and standardisation, though it would probably be true to say that the Calder Valley route retained its essential L&YR character throughout the 1930s – and indeed for many years thereafter.

The Lancashire & Yorkshire system carried large amounts of holiday traffic in the form of excursion trains during the late-summer 'Wakes' holidays. It was usual, at the height of the holiday season, for packed excursions to converge on Blackpool from all over the north of England and later, following the introduction of holidays with pay, whole towns would migrate en masse to Blackpool or other resorts during the one or two-week summer break. In this context, Rochdale, a town of over 90,000 people, generated large amounts of holiday traffic in its own

right, although there were also many extra trains from places such as Burnley, Bradford, and Halifax, many of these workings being routed via Rochdale, Castleton and the Burnley route. At times of exceptional demand, rakes of veteran rolling stock would be hastily assembled to form relief workings, a small pool of obsolescent vehicles being kept in reserve for this specific purpose. In August 1933, *The Railway Magazine* reported that some of these old coaches still carried their original L&YR livery of chocolate below waist height and mid-brown above.

For railway enthusiasts, 'Wakes Week' workings were a source of particular interest, in that all kinds of motive power were pressed into service to cope with the extra demand, and one could never be quite sure what would appear at the head of each packed holiday special! In the 1950s and 1960s, holiday trains from Rochdale, Oldham, Bradford and the neighbouring towns were hauled by any available motive power, including Black Five 4-6-0s, Jubilee 4-6-0s, Royal Scots, Patriots and Britannias, together with Eastern Region classes such as B1 4-6-0s and K3 2-6-0s.

Prior to nationalisation, some of the trans-Pennine services between Manchester and the West Riding were routed via Normanton and the original Manchester & Leeds main line, although many of these workings reached Leeds Central via Laisterdyke and the former Great Northern (later LNER) system. This became the normal route for Calder Valley services during the BR period, and present-day services are routed via Rochdale, Todmorden, Sowerby Bridge, Halifax and Bradford.

MOTIVE POWER IN THE L&YR PERIOD

The Manchester & Leeds Railway was initially worked by Bury-type locomotives, but these diminutive engines, with their bar frames and archaic 'haycock' fireboxes, were rapidly superseded by larger and more powerful 2-2-2, 2-4-0, and 0-6-0 designs.

L&YR Motive Power – Barton Wright 0-6-0 No. 565
Lancashire & Yorkshire Railway Wright 0-6-0 No. 565 was designed by Barton Wright and built by Sharp, Stewart & Co. in 1877 (Works No. 2732). It was rebuilt as an 0-6-0ST in 1891 and withdrawn from service in 1928. Its sister locomotive, No. 957, built in 1887, is now preserved on the Keighley & Worth Valley Railway.

In 1846, the company set up a Locomotive Works at Miles Platting and began building its own locomotives to the designs of engineers such as William Jenkins and William Yates. The L&YR was, at that time, paying high dividends to its shareholders rather than investing in the railway and, in consequence, the locomotive stock became rundown and unable to handle the traffic. There were, nevertheless, a handful of fairly successful classes, including the Jenkins 'Standard Goods' 0-6-0s and the Yates 4 Class 2-4-0s. Many of these engines were later rebuilt as tank engines of various types.

There was an appreciable improvement after 1875, when William Barton Wright (1828–1915) became Locomotive Superintendent, with his predecessor William Yates continuing in service as Works Manager. The Barton Wright–Yates partnership introduced a policy of standardisation, using interchangeable components, together with much improved maintenance and shed facilities. In the next few years, Barton Wright added 450 new locos to the company's stock, his new designs being mainly of the 0-4-4T, 0-6-2T and 0-6-0 type.

In pre-Grouping days, L&YR local passenger services were typically worked by 0-4-4 and 0-6-2 tank engines, with 0-6-0 tender engines on freight duties. The first L&YR 0-4-4Ts were two Kitson-built locomotives and three rebuilt Jenkins 0-6-0 tender engines, and these engines paved the way for the introduction of Barton Wright's G3 Class 0-4-4Ts which worked in the area for many years. Barton Wright's best-known locomotives were perhaps his 0-6-0 goods engines, which were built from 1876 onwards; they had 4 ft 6 in coupled wheels and were popularly known as 'Ironclads' or 'Claddys'. Some of these locomotives were subsequently reconstructed as saddle tanks, in which form numerous examples survived until the British Railways period.

In 1886 William Barton Wright was succeeded as L&YR Chief Mechanical Engineer by John Aspinall (1851–1937), who had previously worked for the Great Southern & Western Railway in Ireland. Aspinall favoured the 2-4-2T wheel arrangement for use on passenger workings over the compact L&YR network. In this context the double-ended 2-4-2T configuration was particularly useful, insofar as engines of this type could run bunker-first without recourse to turning at the end of each journey. A class of 2-4-2T engines was therefore introduced in 1889, the first example being No. 1008. In all, no less than 330 L&YR Radial tanks were built, and over 100 of these useful engines survived into British Railways days. They had 5 ft 8 in coupled wheels and two 17-inch by 26-inch cylinders (later increased to 18 inch by 26 inch). Some examples had lengthened bunkers, and many carried Belpaire boilers. These distinctive and popular L&YR engines remained at work on the L&YR for many years, becoming perhaps the most characteristic passenger locomotives employed on the system.

Aspinall's 27 Class 0-6-0 goods engines were another long-lived L&YR design which had first been introduced in 1889. These locomotives had 5 ft 1 in wheels and 18-inch by 26-inch cylinders, and some examples had Belpaire fireboxes and extended smokeboxes. Numerous Aspinall 0-6-0s survived into the British Railways era, and, in 1960, No. 52322 was restored to its original condition at Horwich Works and sold for private preservation. In addition to his well-known 2-4-2T and 0-6-0 classes, Aspinall also introduced new 4-4-0s for main line passenger work, such as the visually similar 1093 and 1220 Class 4-4-0s, which had unusually large coupled wheels with a diameter of 7 ft 3 in – despite the hilly nature of the Lancashire & Yorkshire system. These 4-4-0 classes can be seen, perhaps, as the progenitors of Aspinall's culminating design – the celebrated 'Highflyer' Atlantics, which retained these huge driving wheels in conjunction with very large, high-pitched boilers.

John Aspinall became L&YR General Manager in 1899, his place as Chief Mechanical Engineer being filled by Albert Hoy, who had previously served as Works Manager at Horwich. 'Harry' Hoy introduced a class of massive 2-6-2Ts for suburban passenger duties, but these were no more effective than the earlier 2-4-2Ts. Hoy was succeeded by George Hughes, who introduced new and more powerful locomotives such as the famous Dreadnought 4-6-0s, which soon became regular performers on the Manchester to Leeds route alongside the Aspinall Atlantics.

On 1 January 1922, the Lancashire & Yorkshire Railway was amalgamated with the London & North Western Railway, while in 1923 the enlarged L&NWR was itself amalgamated with the Midland and other west coast companies to form the London Midland & Scottish Railway. The Grouping inevitably brought rationalisation and standardisation. Locomotives from other constituents of the LMS soon began to appear, together with more modern LMS locomotive designs although, ironically, two of the putative LMS classes which appeared after 1923 were of obvious L&YR ancestry. In 1924, the Hughes Baltic tanks were built at Horwich, the ten 4-6-4Ts being numbered in sequence from 11110 to 11119.

Two years later, in 1926, the first of the Hughes-Fowler 'Crab' Class 2-6-0s emerged from Horwich Works and, like the Hughes 4-6-4Ts, these new moguls were an obvious L&YR design. When first constructed, the Crabs sported full LMS red livery, and they were employed on a wide range of duties including express passenger workings on the Calder Valley route. Later, the Crabs were displaced from Top Link duties following the introduction of Stanier-designed locomotives, but they continued to be widely used on fitted freight workings, semi-fast passenger services and summer excursion services. Other locomotives seen during the LMS era included Black Five 4-6-0s, Stanier Class 8F 2-8-0s, Class 4F 0-6-0s, Class 2P 4-4-0s, Royal Scot 4-6-0s, ex-L&NWR 0-8-0 freight locomotives and large tank engines of various kinds.

RATIONALISATION OF THE SYSTEM

The years following the Second World War were, in many ways, the heyday of the former Lancashire & Yorkshire system. The network was at its very peak in terms of infrastructure, and with a post-war Labour government committed to the idea of an integrated transport system in which railways would play a central role, the future of the system seemed guaranteed. With petrol rationing still in force, the railways remained busy while, for steam enthusiasts, the large numbers of pre-Grouping locomotives still in everyday service were a source of great interest. Unfortunately, the immediate post-war period was marked by a coal crisis, and in these circumstances it was decided that passenger services between Rochdale and Bacup would be withdrawn as a fuel economy measure with effect from 16 June 1947. The last trains ran on Saturday 14 June, the final public service being worked by a Stanier Class 3MT 2-6-2T and two coaches. The closure was confirmed as permanent in 1949.

The election of a Conservative government in 1951 resulted in the lifting of virtually all restrictions on road transport, and within a few years the railways were suffering from the effects of severe competition. The government's response to this unhappy situation was the closure of any part of the railway system that was deemed to be 'uneconomic' – one of the first casualties in the East Lancashire area being the loop line between Great Harwood Junction, Padiham and Rose Grove, which was closed to regular passenger traffic with effect from 2 December 1957, the last trains being run on Saturday

30 December. The line remained in use for Wakes Week traffic until around 1963, while goods were carried until 1964 (when the line was closed to all traffic), apart from coal to Padiham 'B' Power Station, which continued until 1993.

Government hostility towards the nationalised railway system reached its peak in 1963 with the publication of the Beeching Report. Entitled 'The Reshaping of British Railways', this was, in essence, a gigantic closure plan that advocated the withdrawal of passenger services from 5,000 miles of track and the closure of 2,363 stations. As far as the Manchester to Leeds line was concerned, the Beeching Report recommended that the route should be retained, although passenger services would be withdrawn from the Copy Pit line between Todmorden and Rose Grove.

The Beeching programme was rushed into effect, and by September 1964, Transport Minister Ernest Marples had rubber-stamped 129 line closures and refused consent for just ten proposals. However, in October the Labour Party was returned to power with a small majority, and the Beeching closure programme was modified. However, the Labour administration did not halt the closures in their entirety, and the Stubbins to Accrington line was closed with effect from 5 December 1964, while the former Midland line between Skipton and Colne was deleted from the BR network with effect from 2 February 1970.

A significant event amid the general rundown of the 1960s and 1970s was the end of steam operation in August 1968. The Lancashire area saw much activity during the final week of BR steam, with several specials being run on Sunday 4 August. These included a Stephenson Locomotive Society special from Birmingham New Street to Huddersfield that returned via the Copy Pit route behind Stanier Black Five 4-6-0s Nos 44874 and 45017, and a RCTS 'Farewell to Steam' special from Euston that traversed the Skipton to Blackburn line double-headed by Stanier 8F 2-8-0 No. 48476 and BR Standard Class 5MT 4-6-0 No. 73069.

Notwithstanding the general run-down of the railway network during the Beeching period, the train service provided on the Calder Valley route between Manchester and Leeds was still reasonably good; the May 1970 timetable reveals that there were around nineteen trains each way on this former L&YR main line, with additional through services on summer Saturdays to or from destinations such as Blackpool, Liverpool, Southport and Llandudno. The Oldham Loop line was used by around twenty-three trains each way and there were, in addition, a limited number of through trains via the Copy Pit route, including daily through services from Blackpool North to Bradford Exchange and from York to Blackpool North.

The Copy Pit route was run down over the next few years, and by 1982 this former Lancashire & Yorkshire route was being used by just one daily oil train from Immingham to Preston. This residual working was rerouted in 1983, and the Copy Pit line was then closed completely during the summer months.

It appeared that abandonment was merely a formality, but in the event there was an unexpected reprieve. The Burnley Building Society had recently merged with the Bradford-based Provincial Building Society to form the 'National & Provincial'. Following the merger, building society staff were required to travel between the offices in Bradford and Burnley, and an arrangement was therefore made with BR whereby funding would be provided to support a daily train carrying building society staff and internal mail between Preston, Rose Grove and Bradford Interchange. The train, which also carried members of the public, left Preston at 7.18 a.m. and returned from Bradford in the late afternoon; it ran for the first time on 14 May 1984.

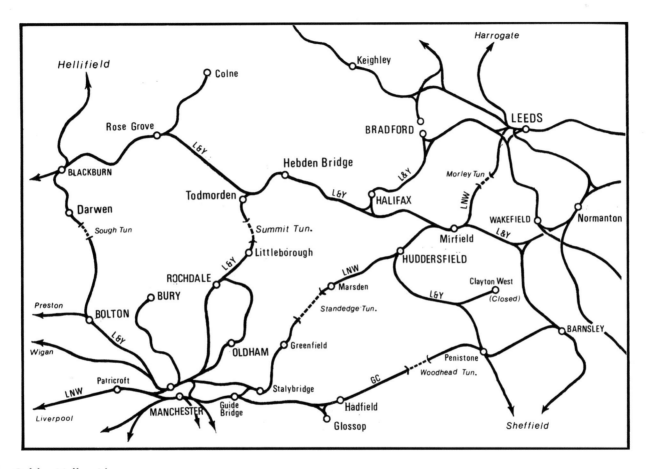

A Map of the Calder Valley Line

This sketch map of the railways between Manchester, Halifax and Leeds shows the present-day Calder Valley route between Manchester, Rochdale, Todmorden, Hebden Bridge, Hallifax, Bradford and Leeds. The original Manchester & Leeds route runs eastwards to Normanton, while the Copy Pit route extends westwards from Todmorden to Rose Grove and Blackburn (the Colne line and the Oldham Loop have now been incorporated into the Manchester Metrolink light railway system).

In October 1984 the revived service was increased to five trains each way between Preston and Leeds, with one service running through to Blackpool North. By May 1988, the service had been increased to eight trains each way, including four that started or terminated their journeys at Blackpool or York. The Manchester & Leeds line has, to some extent, suffered a decline in status, in that the former L&NWR Standage route is now regarded as the principal route between Manchester and the West Riding of Yorkshire. On the other hand, the revival of the Copy Pit route has brought extra traffic to this former L&YR line, which is now enjoying something of a renaissance. Passenger services are now worked by 'second generation' diesel multiple units, including classes 158, 155, 153, 150 and 142, while Class 60 and Class 66 locomotives appear on freight workings.

L&YR Motive Power

Right: Yates 4 Class 2-4-0 No. 51 was built at Miles Platting by the Lancashire & Yorkshire Railway in 1875, and it remained in service until 1894. Some members of this class were built with domed boilers.

Below left: Barton Wright 0-6-2T No. 223 was built by Dübs & Co. in 1883 and withdrawn in 1910.

Below right: This colour-tinted view of an Aspinall 4-4-0 locomotive shows the L&YR's black livery, with red and white lining and brass-beaded splashers; until the 1880s, L&YR locomotives had been painted green.

L&YR Motive Power – The Aspinall 'Atlantics'

Aspinall 4-4-2 No. 1406 was built at Horwich in 1902 as one of a batch of twenty Atlantics (Lot 45) constructed after Alfred Hoy had replaced Aspinall as Chief Mechanical Engineer. It became LMS No. 10321 and remained in service until 1932.

L&YR Motive Power – Passenger Tank Engines

Right: L&YR 243 Class 0-6-2T No. 244 was built by Kitson & Co. in 1881; the engine is shown here as LMS No. 11602.

Below left: Hughes 4-6-4T No. 11117 was built at Horwich in 1924 and withdrawn from service in 1941; only ten of these engines were constructed.

Below right: A broadside view of Aspinall radial 2-4-2T No. 10621. This locomotive was built in 1887 as L&YR No. 1008, but it became LMS No. 10621 at the Grouping and BR No. 50621 following nationalisation. It was withdrawn from active service in 1954 and has now been preserved; as such, it is the only survivor of its once-numerous class.

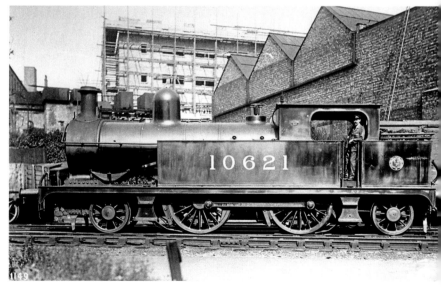

Left: LMS Motive Power

Fowler Class 4MT 2-6-4T No. 42394 at Leeds Holbeck around 1965. Introduced in 1927, the Fowler 2-6-4Ts could easily be distinguished from the Stanier and Fairburn locomotives in that they had Midland-style parallel boilers. Eighteen very similar locomotives were built for service on the LMS system in Northern Ireland.

Right: LMS Motive Power

Fairburn Class 4MT 2-6-4T No. 42052 is photographed in the former Midland Railway shed at Leeds Holbeck, *c.* 1965. These locomotives were introduced in 1945 as a modified version of the slightly earlier Stanier Class 4MT 2-6-4Ts.

Motive Power
A detailed study of Class 5MT 4-6-0 No. 5167 at Leeds Holbeck Shed. The Black Fives were designed by Sir William Stanier (1876–1975) and introduced in 1934. They were among the most successful steam locomotives ever built.

Manchester Victoria
Class 47 locomotive No. 47477 at Manchester Victoria during the 1980s.

Manchester Victoria

As mentioned earlier, the Manchester & Leeds Railway had originally terminated at Oldham Road station in Manchester but, as early as 1839, the company had obtained parliamentary consent for a 'central station' at Hunts Bank that would also be used by the Liverpool & Manchester Railway. The new station, which was linked to the main line by means of a branch from Miles Platting, was opened on 1 January 1844. A few days earlier, a shareholder had suggested that the new station should be called 'Manchester Victoria', which was unanimously agreed, subject to approval by the Liverpool & Manchester Co.

Manchester Victoria was, from its inception, one of the largest stations in the country, although at first, most of the traffic was handled in a single through platform – Leeds trains being dealt with at the east end, while Liverpool & Manchester services used the west end of the station; the platform was 852 feet in length, while the three-span roof covering had an overall length of 700 feet. The facilities soon proved inadequate in relation to ever-increasing traffic requirements and the station was improved and expanded at various times throughout the nineteenth century. A major enlargement scheme was carried out between 1879 and March 1884, as a result of which the station was doubled in size, while on 30 June 1884, the London & North Western Railway opened a separate station known as 'Manchester Exchange'. This new facility was sited to the west of the Lancashire & Yorkshire station, and North Western services gained access from the east via through lines that passed between L&YR platforms 11 and 12.

The upper picture shows the exterior of the 1844 station shortly after opening. Part of this building can still be seen beside the main station building alongside the Hunt's Bank approach road. The lower view shows the transverse 'ridge-and-furrow' overall roof that formerly covered platforms 11 to 16.

Left above: Manchester Victoria – The 1909 Station Building

Further changes were carried out at Manchester Victoria between 1896 and 1909, as a result of which the station acquired a large and impressive four-storey station building flanking the approach road from Long Millgate. Designed by the locally based architect William Dawes, this grandiose structure was built of 'warm grey stone' in a sort of restrained 'Edwardian Baroque' style, which, in the words of *The Manchester Guardian*, was striking 'both as regards design and workmanship'. This still-extant building is sited at right angles to the running lines, and its 480-foot-long façade is graced by an elegant iron and glass canopy which displays the names of an eclectic range of places that could be reached by the Lancashire and Yorkshire Railway – including Scotland, Ireland and Belgium, as well as more obvious destinations such as Liverpool, Bury and Blackpool. The canopy was damaged during the Second World War and by a 1,000 lb IRA bomb on 15 June 1996, but it has since been fully refurbished. The interior arrangements include a row of ornate ticket windows and a huge ceramic map of the Lancashire and Yorkshire Railway system.

Left below: Manchester Exchange

The separate London & North Western Railway station known as Manchester Exchange was sited immediately to the west of Manchester Victoria, on the opposite side of the River Irwell. In LMS days, the need for two entirely separate stations was questioned and the two stations were therefore combined – Platform 3 at Exchange and Platform 11 at Victoria being linked together to form a single through platform, no less than 2,238 feet in length, which was opened on 6 April 1929 and was said to have been the longest in Europe. The combined Victoria and Exchange station was the largest on the LMS system, with twenty-one platform lines, seventeen of which were at Victoria. Manchester Exchange was closed with effect from 5 May 1969 and its buildings were demolished in 1981. Fragments of the platforms remained but, otherwise, most of the steam age infrastructure has been buried beneath the inevitable car parks.

Opposite: Manchester Victoria

Looking eastwards along Platform 11 on 23 July 1983, with Platform 12 visible to the left. Class 25 locomotive No. 25254 is on pilot duty on the centre lines.

Left above: Manchester Victoria – The Concourse
This Edwardian postcard scene is looking northwards along the station concourse, the main station building being to the left, while the suburban platforms can be seen to the right of the picture. Platforms 1, 2 and 3 were adapted for use with the 1,200V DC third rail system in 1917 in order to deal with electrified services on the Bury line; Oldham and Rochdale services normally used Platforms 6, 7 and 8. The concourse is being rebuilt at the time of writing, the most noticeable feature being a striking new glazed roof. Some of the terminal platforms are now used by Metrolink trams.

Left below: Manchester Victoria
Manchester Victoria was formerly served by an electrically powered 'overhead traveller' that extended laterally across the platforms from the parcel office at the north-western corner of the station. Designed by John Aspinall and erected in 1899 by Messrs Mather & Platt, the 'traveller' was suspended from an 11½-inch gauge narrow gauge railway which was fixed to the station roof, and can be soon in the accompanying photograph; the driver rode in a seat beneath the trolley, while parcels were carried in baskets with a length of 5 ft 6 inches and a depth of 3 ft. Sadly, this overhead system was badly damaged during an air raid and it was never repaired. This postcard view of Platform 14 during the early 1900s clearly shows the overhead traveller – which was, in effect, an elevated narrow gauge railway.

Opposite: Manchester Victoria
A further view of the station concourse, with the terminal platforms to the right. The domed refreshment room, which can be seen in the distance (to the left of the clock), has recently been refurbished – the glazed dome has been likened to the dome fitted above the first-class stairway on RMS *Titanic*.

Right: Manchester Victoria – The North Side
Class 40 locomotives Nos 40112 and 40042 were photographed by Roger Sutcliffe at Manchester Victoria in April 1979. Number 40112 is hauling a mixed-freight train, while No. 40053 is being used for station pilot duties.

Left: Manchester Victoria – The North Side
Looking westwards from Platform 11 on 23 July 1983, with Platform 12 visible to the right. The through platforms on the north side of the station were added as part of the 1879–84 enlargement scheme. They were linked to Platform 11 by an underline subway and covered by a 'ridge-and-furrow' overall roof which consisted of a series of transverse 60-ft spans supported on girders and columns. The roof covering between Platforms 11 and 12 was removed in 1924–25, while the ridge-and-furrow roof between Platforms 12 and 16 was partially destroyed by German bombing during the Second World War – Manchester having been the target of a sustained 'Christmas Blitz' on the nights of 22–23 and 23–24 December 1940. Large areas of the city were devastated, leaving an estimated 684 people dead and over 2,300 injured in Manchester, while 215 people were killed and 910 injured in neighbouring Salford.

Right: **Manchester Victoria – The North Side**
Class 47 locomotive No. 47083 waits alongside Platform 14 with a passenger working on 30 June 1979.

Left: **Manchester Victoria – The North Side**
This July 1983 view shows the west end of Platforms 13, 14 and 15, looking east towards the remains of the bomb-damaged ridge-and-furrow roof, which had originally covered a much greater proportion of the platforms. A parcels train is standing in Platform 16, on the extreme left of the picture.

Right: Manchester Victoria – The East End
A detailed study of Manchester Victoria West Signal Box on 6 April 1984.

Opposite: Manchester Victoria
An unidentified Peak Class locomotive stands alongside Platform 12 during the mid-1980s. Platform 12 was used by main-line services to destinations such as Leeds, York and Newcastle. Most of this Victorian infrastructure has now been buried beneath the Manchester Arena.

Left: Manchester Victoria – The East End
Class 45 locomotive No. 45102 departs from Manchester Victoria with an eastbound passenger working during the mid-1980s. Victoria East Junction Signal Box can be seen behind the engine.

Manchester Victoria – Electrification to Bury

In 1844 an undertaking known as 'The Manchester, Bury & Rawtenstall Railway' was incorporated with powers for the construction of a railway commencing at Clifton by a junction with the Manchester & Bolton Railway and terminating at Rawtenstall. After many vicissitudes, the railway was opened throughout to Rawtenstall on 28 September 1846, by which time the Rawtenstall Co. had been amalgamated with the Blackburn, Burnley, Accrington & Colne Railway to form the East Lancashire Railway. The East Lancashire Co. subsequently became part of the Lancashire & Yorkshire Railway and, in 1879, the L&YR opened a new route between Manchester and Bury. The Bury line was electrified in 1916–17 on the 1,200V DC third rail system – platforms 1–3 at Victoria station being adapted for electric operation.

The Rawtenstall line was eventually extended to Bacup, but the local railway system was severely rationalised during the Beeching period and by 1966 the line had been cut back to Rawtenstall, leaving a DMU service between Rawtenstall and Bury – at which point through travellers could change onto the electrified line to Manchester. The Rawtenstall branch was finally closed with effect from 5 June 1972, while the electrified suburban route to Bury was later incorporated into the Manchester 'Metrolink' light railway system. The upper photograph shows a BR Class 504 two-car electric multiple unit at Manchester Victoria with a Bury service, while the colour view shows a 'Victorian mourning party' from the University of Lancaster Transport & Industrial Archaeological Society at Manchester Victoria on Saturday 3 June 1972 – they will shortly be travelling to Bury in order to ride on the last train from Rawtenstall. Happily, the Rawtenstall branch was eventually reopened as the East Lancashire Railway 'heritage' line.

Right: Manchester Victoria

A Swindon-built 'Trans Pennine' unit waits at Manchester Victoria with an Oldham and Rochdale working on 30 June 1979, the leading vehicle being motor composite No. E51962. These six-car units were introduced in 1960, specifically for employment on the long-distance trans-Pennine route between Hull, Leeds, Huddersfield, Stalybridge and Manchester. Each six-car set incorporated two driving motor composites, two motor brake seconds, one trailer second and one trailer first buffet – the four power cars having a total power output of 1,840 bhp. The leading and trailing ends featured semi-streamlined swept-back rooflines and wrap-round windows, which were intended to give these vehicles a 'main line' appearance – although in reality the Trans-Pennine units had a top speed of just 70 mph. These units were designated Class 124 under the BR 'TOPS' scheme and, as such, they remained in service until 1984. None of the Class 124 vehicles have been preserved.

Left: Manchester Victoria

This photograph by Roger Suttcliffe shows Class 45 locomotive No. 45134 waiting at Platform 12 at Manchester Victoria with a through service to Scarborough on 6 April 1984.

Right: Manchester Victoria

Class 40 locomotive No. 40143 is seen at Manchester Victoria with a westbound passenger working on 2 August 1980. Manchester Exchange station be seen in the background.

Opposite: Manchester Victoria

A Class 108 diesel multiple unit led by motor composite No. M54247 No. 45144 at Manchester Victoria on 17 October 1991. Class 142 railbus No. 142030 stands in the adjacent platform.

Left: Manchester Victoria & Manchester Exchange

This *c.* 1970s view is looking westwards from Manchester Victoria towards Manchester Exchange. Manchester Victoria West Junction Signal Box can be seen in the centre of the picture, this 1920s powerbox being similar in appearance to its counterpart at Manchester Victoria East Junction. When brought into use in 1929 as part of the scheme for combining Victoria and Exchange stations, the box had ninety-five levers (including ten spares). The archetypal 1960s tower block that can be seen in the background was erected in 1966 as offices for the Inland Revenue, but in 1998–2000 it was refurbished and adapted for use as a hotel and residential accommodation, the lower portion having become the Manchester Premier Inn, while the upper twelve floors have been turned into flats; the building was originally known as Highland House, but it has now been dubbed The North Tower.

Right: Manchester Victoria
Class 40 locomotive No. 40112 passes through Manchester Victoria with an eastbound freight working in April 1979. These photographs were taken by Roger Suttcliffe.

Opposite: Manchester Victoria
Class 40 locomotive No. 40114 stands alongside Platform 11 on February 1979.

Left: Manchester Victoria
A Metropolitan-Cammell two-car Class 101 multiple unit led by motor brake second No. E50134 is pictured waiting to depart from Manchester Victoria on 21 March 1980, once all of the mail bags have been loaded into the guard's compartment. When first introduced in the mid-1950s, these units were adorned in lined green livery with yellow lining, but this was later replaced by all-over blue, and then by the white-with-blue-stripe colour scheme, as shown in the photograph. This was, in turn, replaced by a more attractive blue and off-white livery scheme.

Left: Manchester Victoria

Gloucester Railway Carriage & Wagon Co. Class 128 motor parcels van No. 55989 at Manchester Victoria on 27 April 1979. The ten members of this class were built in 1959 and remained in service for over thirty years, the last examples being withdrawn for scrapping in 1991. Number 55989 is propelling a former LMS bogie parcels van through the station towards Manchester Exchange.

Right: Manchester Victoria

A general view showing the east end of the station around 1980. Manchester Victoria station was severely rationalised during the 1990s as part of a major city centre redevelopment scheme that was carried out as a corollary of Manchester's bid for the 2000 Olympic Games. In connection with this scheme, the trackwork on the northern side of the station was simplified, and the number of platforms was reduced to just six. At the same time, most of the through tracks were removed, together with former platforms 12 to 17 and their overall roof and platform buildings. In retrospect, this rationalisation of facilities marked the lowest point of the station's fortunes, and in 2013–15 Manchester Victoria was extensively rebuilt and refurbished as part of a much-needed improvement programme.

Opposite: Manchester Victoria – The West End

A view showing the western end of the Manchester Victoria complex, as Class 50 locomotives Nos 50033 *Glorious* and 50007 *Sir Edward Elgar* pass Ordsall Lane Junction, Salford, with the 6.35 a.m. Pathfinder Tours Bristol Temple Meads to Seaforth Docks 'Merseyman' railtour on 30 October 1993. The Granada TV studios can be seen in the background.

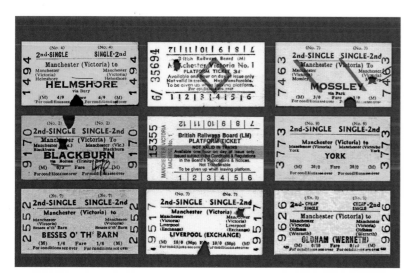

Left above: **Tickets from the Manchester Area**

A selection of nine tickets issued at Manchester Victoria during the British Railways period, including two machine-issued paper platform tickets and seven standard Edmondson card tickets, all of which are second-class singles. Second- and third-class tickets were normally printed on greenish-grey cards during the LMS and BR periods, whereas first-class issues were white. Manchester Victoria continues to be a very busy station, which generated no less than 6,851 million passenger journeys in 2012–13, rising to 7,241 million journeys in 2013–14.

Left below: **Miles Platting**

On leaving Manchester Victoria, 'down' or eastbound trains are faced with rising gradients as steep as 1 in 59 and 1 in 63. This formidable climb was considered to be so arduous that, for a short period during the early days, trains were hauled up to Miles Platting (1½ miles) by a wire cable, although in May 1845 it was reported that this mode of operation had been 'largely discontinued' – ordinary locomotives being used to haul trains up the incline. Miles Platting station (1½ miles), which was opened on 1 January 1844 and closed on Friday 27 May 1995, was the junction for the Oldham Road goods branch and the still-extant branch to Stalybridge, which is used by trains on the former L&NWR 'Standage Route' between Manchester and Leeds. The photograph shows a Cravens Class 108 twin set passing Miles Platting on 21 March 1980, the leading vehicle being motor brake second No. M51938. The unit is wearing the late 1970s refurbished livery of white with a broad blue band. No. M51938 was withdrawn from revenue service in 1992, and it then became departmental unit No. ADB977765.

Opposite: **Miles Platting**

A Derby-built Class 108 two-car unit pauses in the platforms at Miles Platting, the trailing vehicle being motor composite No. 52052.

Right: Miles Platting

A Cravens class 105 twin set with motor composite No. 50805 nearest the camera is pictured at Miles Platting on 21 March 1980. Car No. 50805 was withdrawn just over a year later; in fact the whole class was withdrawn by 1988. The use of asbestos for insulation within the bodywork ensured that very few class 105 vehicles survived into preservation, as it was a condition that the asbestos had to be removed – a very expensive and specialised procedure.

Left: Miles Platting

A Derby class 108 twin car unit led by motor brake second No. M51940 passes Miles Platting on 21 March 1980. This particular vehicle had a lifespan of over three decades, entering service in November 1960, and succumbing to the mass invasion of new Sprinter units in October 1992. It was cut up at MC Metals at Glasgow.

Newton Heath

From Miles Platting the route heads north-eastwards to the next station at Newton Heath (2¾ miles). Opened by the L&YR on 1 December 1853, Newton Heath was the starting point of the 'Oldham Loop', although the junction was to the south of the station, and Oldham services therefore used a separate station that was sited on the loop line and known as 'Dean Lane Newton Heath'. Newton Heath was deleted from the BR system with effect from Monday 3 January 1966, but neighbouring Dean Lane has now been incorporated into the Manchester Metrolink tramway system. The photographs show the station and signal box at Newton Heath, the latter structure being a typical Lancashire & Yorkshire gable-roofed cabin. In steam days, Newton Heath was the site of a large motive power depot, and it is still an important traction maintenance depot. In the 1950s, around 150 locomotives were stationed here, including Jubilee 4-6-0s, Black Five 4-6-0s, Crab 2-6-0s, Class 9F 2-10-0s, WD 2-8-0s, Class 8F 2-8-0s, and the usual range of LMS tank engines and goods locomotives.

Right: **Middleton Junction**

Middleton Junction, the next stopping place (5¼ miles), was opened on
31 March 1842 as the junction for a short branch to Oldham (Werneth).
The station was originally known as 'Oldham Junction', but its name was
changed to 'Middleton Junction' at an early date. On 1 November 1847, the
branch line was extended eastwards from Werneth to Oldham Central and
Oldham Mumps. A second branch was opened from Middleton Junction
to neighbouring Middleton, to the west of the main line, on 1 May 1857.
The accompanying photo shows the main line platforms at Middleton
Junction, looking north, during the early years of the twentieth century;
separate platforms were provided for Werneth branch services. Middleton
Junction East Signal Box can be seen to the right, while the West Box, which
controlled access to the Middleton branch, can be seen in the distance.

Left: **Moston & Mills Hill Stations**

With the adverse gradients easing to 1 in 126, the route continues
north-westwards to Moston (4 miles). Opened in 1872, this suburban
station is situated in a grassy cutting, access from the nearby Hollinwood
Avenue road bridge being by means of sloping ramps. The station is now
an unstaffed halt with simple waiting shelters on each platform. Mills Hill
station, a short distance further on, was first opened in 1839, but it was
closed in 1842, and the present-day stopping place is of comparatively recent
origin, having been opened on 25 March 1985. The station is sited on an
embankment, with steps and sloping ramps from the nearby road.

Left: **The Middleton Branch**

Fairburn Class 4MT 2-6-4T No. 2282 waits in the platforms at Middleton with a local passenger working around 1948. This locomotive became No. 42282 under British Railways' ownership and, as such, it remained in use until final withdrawal in 1964. In 1950, No. 42282 was one of twenty-eight Class 4MT tank locomotives allocated to Newton Heath for local passenger work.

Right: **Middleton Junction**

A general view of Middleton Junction station which, as shown in this old postcard view, was perched on top of an embankment. The Werneth branch was closed to passengers with effect from 9 June 1958, although goods traffic was carried until January 1963. The branch to Middleton was closed with effect from Monday 7 September 1964, while Middleton Junction was itself closed with effect from 3 January 1966 when local stopping services were withdrawn from the Manchester to Todmorden route. As there were no Sunday services, the last trains called on Saturday 1 January 1966.

CASTLETON L & Y. R.

Sear.9 of 105.

Left: Castleton

Castleton, some 9 miles from Manchester Victoria, was opened in 1839, and it became a junction in 1841 when the branch to Heywood was opened. The station, which was sometimes referred to as 'Heywood & Blue Pits', was originally sited on the south side of the Manchester road bridge, but it was rebuilt on the north side of the bridge around 1875. Up and down platforms were provided here, the main station building being on the up side, while the two slightly staggered platforms were connected by a lattice girder footbridge. The now closed Heywood to Bolton line joined the Calder Valley route by means of a triangular junction on the south side of the Manchester road bridge, the line being retained for freight traffic after the cessation of passenger services in 1970. In recent years, this closed line has been used for movements of locomotives and rolling stock to and from the East Lancashire Railway which, in September 2003, opened an extension to Heywood.

Right: Castleton

The area around Castleton station was heavily industrialised, and a number of large textile mills could be seen on each side of the line. Some of these premises, such as the extensive Dunlop Cotton Mills on the down side of the line, were served by private sidings. Other rail-linked firms in the vicinity included Messrs Magee, Marshall & Co., a well-known local brewing firm, and the Wigan Coal Corporation between Rochdale and Castleton. This old postcard view is looking north towards Rochdale during the early years of the twentieth century, as an Aspinall 2-4-2T approaches the crowded up platform with a southbound passenger train; Magee Marshalls' maltings can be seen just beyond the station. Castleton has now been reduced to unstaffed halt status, with modern waiting shelters on each platform.

CASTLETON STATION.

FRESHMENT ROOM

ROCHDALE STATION.

Left: Rochdale Station

On departing from Castleton, trains run north-eastwards to Rochdale (10½ miles) on a gently rising gradient of 1 in 330. When first opened in 1839, Rochdale station had consisted of a 'small, but commodious and neat edifice', but in the fullness of time the original facilities became inadequate, and it was therefore decided that the station would be reconstructed on a new site, some twenty-six chains to the south-west. This work was under way by 1887 and the new station was officially opened on 28 April 1889. The rebuilt station incorporated twin island platforms and a connecting subway. The up island was equipped with two bay platforms at its west end, while the down island was similarly equipped with two bays at its eastern end. With a length of 1,281 feet, the down platform was one of the longest on the Lancashire & Yorkshire system, while the underline subway had a width of 21 feet.

Right: Rochdale Station

The up and down platforms were covered by hipped-roof glass-and-iron canopies, and substantial station buildings were provided on both sides – the main building, on the west side, having a small clock tower. In LMS days, the main booking office was known as the 'A' office, while a subsidiary booking office on the east side of the station was known as the 'B' office.

Rochdale's original station was relegated to the status of a goods depot after 1889, although the old station building remained in use as offices. Over fifty sidings were available for goods traffic or marshalling purposes, in addition to various carriage sidings and refuge roads. The infrastructure included a large cotton warehouse, while an 'accumulator house' contained hydraulic equipment to drive cranes, shunting capstans and the station lifts. The most powerful crane had a lifting capacity of 10 tons.

LANCASHIRE AND YORKSHIRE RAILWAY

ROCHDALE STATION

ROCHDALE RY STATION.   T. PINDER, PHO

Right: Rochdale

This old photograph was taken from an unusual vantage point at the bottom of one of the subway stairwells. A considerable number of people have assembled at the top of the stairs, suggesting that a special event was taking place – could this photograph have been taken during the opening of the new station in 1889?

Opposite: Rochdale

A detailed study of the main station building, which was situated at street level and was connected to the platforms by the subway.

Left: Rochdale Station

A further view of the platforms during the early years of the twentieth century. In 1932, *The LMS Railway Magazine* stated that, on weekdays, Rochdale station was handling ninety-five arrivals and seventy-seven departures from the up platform, and seventy arrivals and eighty-nine departures from the down platform. It is interesting to note that the area immediately to the north of the goods yard was associated with the popular music hall entertainer and film star Dame Gracie Fields (1898–1979), who had been born at No. 9 Molesworth Street, the eldest of the four children of Fred Stansfield, an engineer, and his wife, Sarah Jane Bamford.

Right: Rochdale – Some Suburban Tickets

A selection of Edmondson card tickets from various stations on the western section of the Calder Valley route between Manchester Victoria and Todmorden, including Manchester Victoria, Miles Platting, Walsden, Castleton, Smithy Bridge and Todmorden. Most of these tickets are standard British Railways issues, but the privilege ticket from Smithy Bridge (No. 1212) is an LMS ticket, and the third-class single from Todmorden to Burnley (No. 3664) dates back to the days of the Lancashire & Yorkshire Railway ('privilege tickets' were reduced fare tickets issued to railwaymen and members of their families). Many of the tickets issued by British Railways had red overprints: 'R', for example, denoted a return ticket, while a red 'D' signified that the ticket was a cheap day return.

Left: Rochdale

The infrastructure at Rochdale was rationalised during the 1960s and 1970s, Milnrow Road goods yard being closed in 1968, while further alterations were put into effect in April 1978, when work started on a £200,000 reconstruction scheme. Extensive track and signalling alterations were carried out so that passenger trains to Manchester, Oldham, Leeds and Bradford could use one of the island platforms and one bay. The new works included 'a concrete raft', which was erected over the existing stairwell on the surviving island platform in order to provide support for a new building containing the ticket and parcels offices. Further along the platform, a new waiting room and toilets were provided, while the remaining buildings were refurbished. Sadly, the low-level station building shown in the accompanying photograph has been demolished.

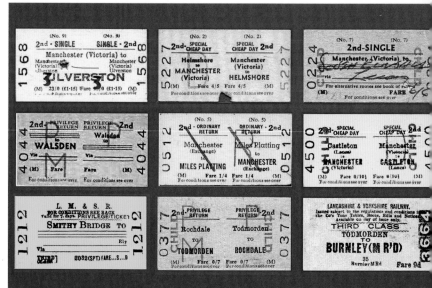

Central Station. Oldham.

Right above: The Oldham Loop – Oldham Central

As mentioned in the historical section, the Oldham Loop was opened in stages, the centre section between Oldham Werneth and Oldham (Mumps) having been part of the original Oldham branch from Middleton Junction, while the northern section from Oldham (Mumps) to Rochdale East Junction was opened on 2 November 1863. The southern section from Oldham Werneth to Thorpes Bridge Junction was completed on 17 April 1880, and Oldham was thereby placed on a through route between Manchester, Oldham and Rochdale, which ran more or less parallel to the main line, and developed as an important suburban route. Oldham Central station was situated in a cutting with substantial buildings on both sides, while the platforms were covered, for much of their length, by 'ridge-and-furrow' canopies. Oldham Clegg Street, the former Oldham, Ashton & Guide Bridge station, was situated on an adjoining site – the two stations forming, in effect, a 'V'-shaped junction with two sets of converging platforms. Oldham Clegg Street, which was opened on 26 August 1861 and substantially reconstructed around 1900, boasted an island platform and a flanking side platform.

Right below: The Oldham Loop – New Hey

The Oldham Loop had intermediate stations at Dean Lane, Failsworth, Hollinwood, Werneth, Oldham Central, Oldham Mumps, Royton Junction, Shaw & Crompton, New Hey and Milnrow. New Hey, some 12 miles to the north of Manchester Victoria, was opened on 2 November 1863 and closed on Saturday 3 October 2009, so that the line could be electrified and adapted for use as part of the Manchester Metrolink system. Goods facilities were withdrawn in October 1966, and the station became an unstaffed halt in September 1969. The Manchester 'Metrolink' system was developed in stages throughout the 1990s, and at the end of the decade it was decided that the former Oldham Loop would be adapted for use as an electrified light railway, with trams running through from Rochdale to central Manchester. The proposed light railway would, in general, follow the existing 'heavy rail' route, albeit with deviations through the town centres of Rochdale and Oldham. New Hey was reopened as a Metrolink stop on 28 (23?) February 2013 and, in its present-day-form the station is served by five trams per hour between Rochdale, Manchester and East Didbury.

Left above: The Oldham Loop – Milnrow

Milnrow, some 12¾ miles miles from Manchester Victoria, was the last stopping place before Rochdale. It was opened on 2 November 1863, closed in October 2009, and reopened as a Metrolink station on 28 February 2013. It had been reported at the time that the new light railway would be opened as far as Oldham in 2011, although problems with the computerised control system caused considerable delays and, in the event, the new Metrolink line was not completed throughout to Rochdale until 23 February 2013.

Left below: The Oldham Loop – The Royton Branch

The Oldham Loop was the starting point for a branch from Royton Junction to Royton. This short line, a little over 1 mile in length, was opened on 21 March 1864 and closed with effect from Monday 18 April 1966. Royton Junction was a passenger-only station with no public goods handling facilities, but it was lavishly equipped with an array of parallel goods sidings on the up side, while further sidings were available to the north of the station on the down side of the Rochdale line. These sidings were used mainly for marshalling and stabling purposes, but they were particularly useful during the annual Oldham Wakes holidays, when the railways were hard-pressed to move huge numbers of holidaymakers to and from their chosen seaside destinations. Rakes of spare coaches would often be assembled in the sidings prior to the Wakes, in order that a sufficient supply of rolling stock would be available to accommodate all of those wishing to migrate to the seaside. The photograph provides a glimpse of the branch line terminus at Royton around 1910.

Opposite: The Oldham Loop – Royton

A Class 108 unit stands alongside the rainswept platform at Royton. In contrast to neighbouring Royton Junction, Royton was able to handle public goods traffic, its goods yard being equipped with a range of facilities including coal wharves, cattle loading pens ad a 5-ton yard crane.

Left above: The Oldham Loop – Some Suburban Tickets

A selection of British Railways and LMS tickets from Oldham (Mumps) and local stations on the Oldham Loop, including Dean Lane, New Hey, Milnrow, Oldham Central, Royton and Royton Junction. Most of these stopping places have now been incorporated into the Manchester Metrolink light railway system.

Left below: The Bacup Branch

The Bacup branch ran north-westwards from Rochdale to Wardleworth, then northwards via Shawclough & Healey (3 miles), Broadley (3¾), Whitworth (4½ miles) and Facit (5¾ miles). Beyond, the heavily graded line continued to Shawforth (6¾ miles), where several private sidings were situated. Trains were then faced with a 1 in 39 rising gradient as far as the Britannia Quarry siding, which marked the summit of the line – 967 feet above mean sea level and the highest point on the L&YR system. Britannia station, which opened in 1881, had a comparatively short life as it was closed to public traffic in 1917, although it is believed that workmen's trains continued to call. The final section involved a 1 in 34 descent into Bacup, where the branch converged with an earlier line from Rawtenstall. Bacup station, opened on 1 October 1852, boasted a double-sided terminal platform, a fully equipped goods yard and a four-road engine shed.

The steep gradients on the Bacup branch contributed to a serious accident that took place on Saturday 29 August 1891, when a runaway goods train composed of twenty-five heavily laden stone wagons collided with an up passenger train at Facit, resulting in two fatalities and many injuries. Passenger services between Rochdale and Bacup were withdrawn in 1947, but the branch was used for freight traffic for many years and the final section did not close until August 1967. The accompanying picture provides a panoramic view of Bacup goods yard around 1900.

Littleborough

From Rochdale, the Manchester & Leeds main line continues along dead-level alignments to Smithy Bridge, some 12 miles 60 chains from Manchester Victoria. This small station was opened by the L&YR in 1868 and closed with effect from 2 May 1960. However, it was later decided that Smithy Bridge would be resurrected, and a new station was officially opened on 19 August 1985, the opening ceremony being attended by civic dignitaries from Manchester and West Yorkshire, together with local Members of Parliament. The new station, which was funded by the Greater Manchester Council, consists of timber trestle platforms, with small shelters on each side. The platforms are slightly staggered, while a minor road crosses the line at the north end of the station. The signal cabin survived as a gate box until 2014, but this standard L&YR structure has now been demolished.

Curving onto a north-easterly heading, trains faced gradients of 1 in 336 and 1 in 330, which continue through Littleborough (13¾ miles) towards Summit Tunnel. Littleborough station was opened on 3 July 1839, and it served as a temporary terminus until the line was completed throughout on 1 March 1841. The layout here consists of staggered up and down platforms, Platform 2, the down or eastbound platform, being further along the line towards Leeds than Platform 1. The station building is on the down side, and the platforms are linked by a subway. The ticket office and waiting room are still in use and, in addition, both platforms are equipped with waiting shelters. The picture to the right shows Littleborough Signal Box, while the lower view shows part of the station building.

Littleborough

Left above: Situated around a mile beyond Littleborough station, the 2,885-yard Summit Tunnel is preceded by the 44-yard Summit East Tunnel and a deep cutting, as shown in this photograph of Class 50 locomotive No. 50031 *Hood* approaching the East Tunnel in pouring rain while hauling the 6.55 a.m. Pathfinder Tours 'Whistling Scotsman' railtour on 26 August 2005. This enthusiasts' special ran from Birmingham New Street to Kyle of Lochalsh, the Class 50 being used as far as Bradford, where it was replaced by Class 40 locomotive No. 40145. As its name implies, the tunnel marks the summit of the Manchester & Leeds route, and trains enter the south (Littleborough) portal on a rising gradient of 1 in 330, and emerge from the north portal on a falling gradient of 1 in 182. The tunnel is virtually dead straight, with a slight westwards curve at the north end, while the brick lining, which extends throughout the length of the bore, is of up to six courses.

Left below: Class 158 unit No. 158756 emerges from Summit Tunnel while forming the 7.18 a.m. Leeds to Manchester Victoria Northern Rail service on 16 March 2015. The Littleborough portal, which can be seen behind the train, is superbly built in high-quality masonry. The Calder Valley route has always been an important route for bulk freight traffic such as oil from Billingham to Manchester. On 20 December 1984, a train carrying 243,000 gallons of petrol became derailed while passing through Summit Tunnel, and although Class 47 locomotive No. 47125 and three 100-ton bogie tank wagons were rescued, around 186,000 tons of petrol ignited, causing a major fire. At the height of the conflagration, flames burst 250 feet from the ventilation shafts, although the resulting damage to George Stephenson's strongly built tunnel was not as serious as had been feared, and the Manchester to Leeds route was brought back into full use after repairs to the damaged portion of the tunnel lining had been carried out.

Opposite: Walsden

Running 50 minutes early, Class 56 locomotive No. 56078 *Doncaster Enterprise* heads through typical Pennine scenery at Walsden with the Pathfinder Tours 'Twilight Grids' railtour on 31 March 2004. This was a sad day for Class 56 fans, as it was marked the end of the class' service on the national rail network.

Left above: Walsden

Having emerged from Summit Tunnel, trains pass through the 44-yard Summit West Tunnel and then head northwards along a narrow valley that they share with the Rochdale Canal and the A6033 road. Falling at 1 in 182, the railway passes through the 306-yard Winterbutlee Tunnel before trains reach the next stopping place at Walsden, 17¾ miles 70 chains from Manchester. This station was opened in 1845 and closed with effect from 6 August 1961 but, like Smithy Bridge, it was subsequently reopened – the new facilities being brought into use on 10 September 1990. The present station has slightly staggered up and down platforms, and it is sited a short distance to the north of the original stopping place.

Left below: Todmorden

Still descending at 1 in 181, the route turns onto a north-easterly heading as it follows the valley towards Todmorden, 19 miles 13 chains from Manchester. Opened in January 1841, Todmorden station became the junction for the Copy Pit line in November 1849. The Copy Pit route joins the main line by means of a triangular junction to the north of Todmorden station – a west curve being provided to facilitate through running between Burnley, Todmorden and Manchester, while an east-to-west curve is available for through services between Yorkshire and Lancashire that do not call at Todmorden. The south-to-west connection between Todmorden East Junction and Stansfield Hall Junction was lifted following the withdrawal of local services in 1965, but it has latterly been reinstated, the first train to use the rebuilt west curve being an enthusiasts' special arranged by Pathfinder Tours on 31 May 2014. The photograph shows Class 158 unit No. 158843 on the direct east-to-west arm of the triangle with the 9.11 a.m. Blackpool North to York Northern service on 16 November 2015.

Opposite: Todmorden

An atmospheric view of Todmorden station during the L&YR period, probably taken around 1912.

Todmorden

Left above: Prior to rationalisation, the infrastructure at Todmorden had consisted of up and down platforms for passenger traffic, with an additional bay for local services to and from Rose Grove. The platforms were linked by an underline subway and there were substantial station buildings on both sides, the main buildings being on the up side. The nearby goods sidings could deal with all forms of traffic including coal, furniture, livestock, road vehicles, horse boxes and general merchandise, while a 10-ton yard crane was available for loading large or heavy consignments. Todmorden has retained much of its Victorian infrastructure, although the platform canopies have been removed and the goods yard was closed in 1972. The accompanying picture is a postcard view of Todmorden Viaduct, to the east of the station.

Left below: Class 150 units Nos 150112 and 150215 approach Hall Royd Junction, at the eastern corner of the Todmorden triangle, while forming the late-running 10.16 a.m. Manchester Victoria to Leeds service on 16 November 2015. This panoramic view of Todmorden is dominated by the impressive town hall, which was built in 1875 and can be seen in the centre of the picture. The railway station can be glimpsed to the right of the town hall, while the west curve from Stansfield Hall Junction can be seen on the extreme right. This reinstated connection has enabled direct services to be reintroduced between Burnley and Manchester via the Copy Pit route.

Opposite: Todmorden

Class 155 unit No. 155345 passes Hall Royd Junction with the 9.26 a.m. Leeds to Manchester Victoria service on 16 November 2015. Millwood Tunnel is visible in the background, while the Stoodley Pike monument that can be seen on the distant hilltop commemorates the surrender of Paris and the defeat of Napoleon at the Battle of Waterloo in 1815 – the present monument having been erected in 1856 to replace an earlier monument that had fallen down after a lightning strike.

Todmorden

Left above: A hybrid four-car diesel multiple unit formation consisting of Class 150 unit No. 15070 and Class 142 two-car railbus set No. 142027 rounds the east curve between Todmorden East Junction and Hall Royd Junction while forming the 9.16 a.m. Manchester Victoria to Leeds service on 16 November 2015. The reinstated west curve between Todmorden East Junction and Stansfield Hall Junction can be seen disappearing behind the silver birch trees in the background. All of the 'second generation' multiple units can be coupled together and worked in multiple by a single driver.

Left below: Class 158 unit No. 158758 takes the eastern arm of the Todmorden triangle as it passes Hall Royd Junction with the late-running 9.19 a.m. Leeds to Manchester Victoria service on 16 November 2015; the train is slowing down prior to entering Todmorden station, a short distance further on. Built at Derby Carriage & Wagon Works between 1989 and 1992, the Class 158 sets are generally considered to be the most comfortable of the 'second generation' BR multiple units. They are fully air-conditioned, and have a top speed of 90 mph.

Opposite: Todmorden

Freightliner Class 66 locomotive No. 66525 passes Hall Royd Junction on 16 November 2015 with the 5.45 a.m. Immingham to Fiddlers Ferry imported coal train. This was a slightly unexpected working, as there was no mention of it on the Realtime Trains website, not even as a cancellation.

Eastwood

Beyond Todmorden, the railway runs through a narrow valley, tunnelling through several rocky outcrops in a manner reminiscent of some of the lines in the mountainous areas of France. The tunnels on this section include Millwood Tunnel, Horsfall Tunnel and Castle Hill Tunnel, which have lengths of 225 yards, 264 yards, and 198 yards respectively. Eastwood station (21½ miles) was opened January 1841 and closed with effect from 3 December 1951. The photograph, taken from an elevated position, reveals that this abandoned station consisted of staggered up and down platforms, separated by an intervening level crossing. The station building was a small, cottage-type structure, while the goods yard could deal with coal-class traffic and general merchandise.

Opposite: Todmorden

Colas Rail Freight Class 60 locomotive No. 60096 rounds the sharp curve between Stansfield Hall Junction and Hall Royd Junction while hauling the 8.55 a.m. Preston Docks to Lindsey Oil Refinery empty bitumen tanks on 16 November 2015. This was taken when the sun was at a perfect angle, just glancing across the front of the locomotive.

Hebden Bridge

Left above: Falling at 1 in 179, the railway passes through the 109-yard Weasal Hall Tunnel before trains come to rest at Hebden Bridge, 23 miles 50 chains from Manchester. This station was opened on 5 October 1840 and it has staggered up and down platforms – the down platform being further to the east than its counterpart on the up side of the line. There are extensive, stone buildings on each side, and the platforms are linked by an underline subway with sloping ramps. The main station building, on the down side, dates from around 1893, and the platforms have retained their traditional glass and iron canopies with fretwork valancing. The goods yard, now removed, was situated to the west of the passenger station on the down side, and its facilities included a goods shed, coal sidings, cattle loading pens and a 10-ton yard crane. The track layout has now been reduced to a single crossover, with a dead-end siding on the down side. The photograph shows Class 158 unit No. 158757 arriving at Hebden Bridge while working the 12.18 a.m. Leeds to Manchester service on 16 March 2015.

Left below: A panoramic view of Hebden Bridge, looking south towards the station during the early years of the twentieth century. The railway, the River Calder and the Rochdale Canal are hemmed-in by the Pennines, which rise to around 1,500 feet, with mills and houses clinging grimly to the hillsides. Although the layout at Hebden Bridge has obviously been rationalised, the station was attractively restored in 1981, complementing efforts that were being made elsewhere in the town. The refurbishment included a repainting of the station in the chocolate and white colours of the former Lancashire & Yorkshire Railway – the efforts that had been made in connection with the restoration scheme being acknowledged by the Chairman of the Calder Civic Trust, who presented the BR Area Manager with a small plaque.

Opposite: Hebden Bridge

Class 158 unit No. 158906 approaches the down platform at Hebden Bridge while forming the 12.26 p.m. Manchester Victoria to Leeds Northern Rail service on 16 March 2015. This view clearly shows the station's staggered up platform.

THE STATION HEBDEN BRIDGE.

Left above: **Hebden Bridge – The Main Station Building**
A detailed view of the main station building, which replaced an earlier structure in 1893. The central part of the building boasts a French-style Mansard roof, which is perhaps a somewhat unexpected feature in the Calder Valley. The one-and-a-half-storey centre clock is flanked by two single-storey wings, both of these being hip-roofed. Internally, the building, now Grade II listed, contains a ticket office, a booking hall, a general waiting room and a ladies' waiting room, together with a coffee bar and a private day nursery. Additional waiting rooms are available on the up platform.

Left below: **Hebden Bridge – The Signal Cabin**
A detailed view of the standard Lancashire & Yorkshire Railway signal box, which was built in 1891 and is sited to the east of the platforms on the down side. The cabin, now a Grade II-listed building, retains its original thirty-six-lever frame (with two more recent additions) and is one of the best surviving examples of a L&YR box. The signal box was refurbished in 2007, and work carried out at that time included the provision of an inside toilet for the signalman, which was built in the style of an original water closet. The signal box is pictured here on 16 March 2015.

Opposite: **Hebden Bridge**
A further view of Hebden bridge station, looking west towards Manchester Victoria from the up platform. This recent photograph, taken on 16 March 2015, provides a good view of the glazed platform canopies, which are supported on cast-iron posts and have geometrical ornamentation in their spandrels.

Hebden Bridge from Wood Top

Left: **Hebden Bridge**

Another panoramic view of the station and goods yard, showing how the railway shares the narrow valley with houses, roads, mills and the canal. The passenger station can be seen in the centre of the picture, with the large goods shed to the left.

Right: **Hebden Bridge – The 1912 Derailment**

Hebden Bridge was the setting for an accident that took place on 21 June 1912 when the 2.25 p.m. express from Manchester to Leeds left the rails at Charlestown Curve, on the approaches to the station, resulting in the deaths of four passengers and injuries to another sixty-three people, including the driver, fireman and guard. The train consisted of six passenger vehicles and a six-wheeled luggage van, being used as a hearse, while the engine was a 2-4-2T. In giving evidence at the inquest on the four victims, the driver, George Medley, said that the engine and the first coach left the rails, while 'the second coach, containing the corpse, seemed to be a proper wreck, and the third was turned on its side'. The rear coaches remained on the rails, and the uninjured passengers were able to help with the rescue of their fellow travellers. Lieutenant-Colonel Druitt RE, of the Board of Trade, attributed the accident to the employment of a 2-4-2T tank engine at too high a speed on a curve of 30-chain radius.

Right: Mytholmroyd

An old postcard view of Mytholmroyd, with the station building visible to the right of the picture. The upper floor contained a waiting room, while the platform frontage featured a full-length hip-roofed canopy supported by decorative fretted brackets at eaves level. The platforms are now equipped with glazed waiting shelters which, though of recent construction, are gable-roofed structures of fairly substantial design.

Left: Mytholmroyd

Running through a sylvan landscape, dominated by Midgley Moor, trains reach the wayside station at Mytholmroyd (24¾ miles), which was opened in 1847 and is situated on a viaduct. Up and down platforms are provided here, the main station building being on the down side, while the up platform was originally equipped with a small, hip-roofed waiting room. Although the station building appears to be a squat, hip-roofed structure, this circa-1912 postcard view is deceptive, as the building was in fact a three-storey split-level structure incorporating a booking hall and an internal stairway – the building being, in effect, a stair tower. This interesting structure is out of use at the time of writing, but efforts are being made to restore it to its former glory. Access to the platforms is now by means of steps and sloping ramps – the old station building having been sealed-up in an attempt to deter vandals.

Mytholmroyd

Right above: An Edwardian postcard view showing a Lancashire &
Yorkshire express passenger working hurrying through Mytholmroyd
station. The locomotive has a Belpaire boiler and distinctive windows in
its cab front, suggesting that it is an Aspinall Atlantic.

Right below: A four-car formation comprising Class 150 unit
No. 150215 and sister unit No. 150112 enters the up platform at
Mytholmroyd while working the 8.26 a.m. Leeds to Manchester Victoria
service on 16 November 2015. The leading unit is sporting a 'Movember'
moustache, raising awareness of men's heath issues, while the prominent
'Connecting the North' banner on the opposite platform is adorned with
silhouettes of various northern landmarks, including the Angel of the
North. The station is supported by a very active passengers' user group
known as 'The Mytholmroyd Station Partnership', which has enhanced
the platforms by the provision of gardens, flower tubs and school art –
including 'The Northern Mosaic' by students from Calder High School.
In recent years, Mytholmroyd has generated around 158,000 million
passenger journeys per annum.

Opposite: Mytholmroyd

Running 32 minutes late due to flooding caused by the previous day's
torrential rain, Class 158 unit No. 158757 arrives at Mytholmroyd
station with the 8.16 a.m. Manchester Victoria to Leeds Northern service
on 16 November 2015.

Left above: Mytholmroyd

The four-car Class 150 formation, seen on the previous page, is here departing from Mytholmroyd station on 16 November 2015, with unit No. 150112 at the rear. Note the absence of a corridor connection – No. 150112 being a Class 150/1, whereas No. 150215, the leading unit, is composed of two Class 150/2 vehicles.

Left below: Luddendenfoot

Now heading south-eastwards, the route continues its gradual descent towards Luddendenfoot station (26½ miles), which was opened on 5 October 1840 and closed with effect from 10 September 1962. On a literary note, it is interesting to recall that Branwell Brontë (1817–48), the dissolute brother of novelists Emily, Charlotte and Anne, was employed as assistant 'clerk-in-charge' at Sowerby Bridge station in October 1840 and, in the following year, he was transferred to Luddendenfoot as a clerk-in-charge at an increased salary of £130 per annum. Sadly, in March 1862, a subordinate was discovered to have stolen £11 1s 7d from the railway company and although the unfortunate Branwell was not suspected of theft, he was held to have been responsible and was dismissed from the company's service. The picture shows Luddenfoot station during the pre-Grouping period, around 1912.

Luddendenfoot

The right-hand picture shows Class 158 unit No. 158755 passing a fine
display of autumnal foliage, as it enters the deep cutting near Luddendenfoot
while forming the 7.51 a.m. Leeds to Manchester Victoria Northern service
on 16 November 2015. Sowerby's eighteenth-century parish church can
be glimpsed on the distant horizon. The lower view shows Class 155 unit
No. 155345 in the same cutting with the 7.48 a.m. Manchester Victoria to
Leeds service. In common with many other trains in the Pennines area on
that date, the train had been delayed by flooding – indeed water can be seen
cascading down the side of the cutting on the left of the picture, although in
this case the excess water was able to drain away.

Left above: Luddendenfoot

A final glimpse of Luddendenfoot station during the early years of the twentieth century, showing the staggered platforms and road overbridge.

Left below: Sowerby Bridge

Continuing south-eastwards, trains pass through the 657-yard Sowerby Bridge Tunnel before reaching the still-extant station at Sowerby Bridge (28½ miles). This station was opened on 5 October 1840 and rebuilt on a new site some 28 chains further east in 1876 – a contract for the new works being let on 25 June 1873 at a cost of £25,634. Although now reduced to just two staggered platforms, the infrastructure here was once extensive, with additional platforms on the up side and a terminal bay on the down side of the station, together with a motive power depot and the usual goods facilities. The 1938 Railway Clearing House *Handbook of Stations* reveals that Sowerby Bridge could handle all kinds of goods traffic, including coal, vehicles, livestock, furniture and general merchandise traffic. The coal drops that lined Station Road were an interesting feature, insofar as they were situated beneath the arches of a viaduct. There were, in addition, several private sidings, including J. Clay & Son's Siding, the Co-operative Wholsale Siding, J. Shaw & Son's Siding, Shepherd & Blackburn's Siding, and the Hollings Mill Estate Co. Siding.

Opposite: Sowerby Bridge – The Main Station Building

This hand-tinted Edwardian postcard shows the main station building, which was situated on the up side. The building was an L-shaped structure, with its main block at right angles to the platforms and a single-storey wing that was parallel to the running lines. In October 1978 the building was damaged by fire, the alarm having been raised by a policeman at 2.00 a.m., who alerted the local fire brigade. The firefighters managed to save much of the 102-year-old structure, but the building was then left in a derelict condition. The Sowerby Bridge Civic Society hoped that the building could be listed for its historical and architectural importance, but BR nevertheless demolished the main portion in November 1980, leaving the single-storey wing in situ. The station is now unstaffed, but the surviving part of the station building has found a new role as a popular and successful pub and restaurant known as The Jubilee Refreshment Rooms.

Right: Sowerby Bridge – The Signal Box
A detailed study of Sowerby Bridge West Box, which was a standard Lancashire & Yorkshire Railway gable-roofed brick-and-timber structure with its glazed upper floor 'jetted out' from the brick-built locking room. The box was damaged by fire on 15 June 1984, and closed in May 1985 when the absolute block section was extended. The eastern portal of Sowerby Bridge Tunnel can be seen in the background.

Left: Sowerby Bridge
A general view of the station in the Edwardian period. Sowerby Bridge motive power depot was sited to the west of the passenger station on the down side of the running lines. It was coded '25E' from 1948 until 1956, and '56E' thereafter, and normally housed around thirty locomotives. The shed building incorporated six roads, while the usual coaling and watering facilities were available. In March 1938 *The Railway Magazine* reported that a new turntable with a diameter of 60 feet was being installed at Sowerby Bridge in order to accommodate Black Five 4-6-0s and other large engines that were then being introduced. In 1959, the locally based engines included eight WD Class 2-8-0s, four Fairburn Class 4MT 2-6-4Ts, three Fowler Class 4MT 2-6-4Ts, one Ivatt Class 6P/5F 2-6-0, one Stanier Class 3MT 2-6-2T, five Fowler Class 3F 0-6-0Ts and four ex-Lancashire & Yorkshire Class 3F 0-6-0s. The shed was closed in 1964.

Sowerby Bridge – The Rishworth Branch

Sowerby Bridge was formerly the junction for branch line services to Rishworth that ran southwards over a 3¾-mile branch which had originally been planned as part of an alternative route to Rochdale. Although the scheme was first put forward during the 'Railway Mania' years of the 1840s, nothing tangible was achieved until 5 July 1865, when the L&YR obtained parliamentary consent for the proposed line. In the event, construction did not begin until September 1873 and the first section was not opened until 5 August 1878, when passenger services started running between Sowerby Bridge and Ripponden, a distance of 2 miles 73 chains. The line was finally completed throughout to Rishworth on 1 March 1881.

The Rishworth branch commenced 9 chains to the east of Sowerby Bridge station, the junction being facing to the direction of down trains, which meant that a reversal was necessary for trains proceeding to and from the main line station. This mode of operation continued until 1 March 1907, when steam railmotors were introduced, and a separate branch platform was brought into use at Sowerby Bridge. The Rishworth branch was closed to passengers on Saturday 6 July 1929, but goods traffic was handled at Rishworth until February 1953, and at Ripponden until September 1958, when the line was closed to all traffic. The upper photograph shows a Lancashire & Yorkshire Railway steam railmotor at Sowerby Bridge, while the lower view provides a general view of Ripponden station, which occupied a shelf on the side of a hill.

Left: The Rishworth Branch – Watson's Crossing Halt

The Rishworth branch was double-tracked throughout, with a 593-yard tunnel at the north end of the line near Sowerby Bridge, and intermediate stopping places at Watson's Crossing, Triangle and Ripponden. The photograph shows the very basic passenger facilities at Watson's Crossing Halt, which was brought into use in conjunction with the introduction of steam railmotor services on 1 March 1907. By 1921, Watson's Crossing and the other stations on the Rishworth branch were being served by eighteen around trains each way. Sadly, this very respectable service was unable to save the line from closure at the end of the decade – the main reason for the loss of passenger traffic being the introduction of rival motor bus services between Halifax and Rishworth.

Right: The Rishworth Branch – Triangle

Triangle station was opened by the L&YR on 1 June 1885. It served the nearby village of Triangle, which is said to have derived its name from a patch of ground at the divergence of the old and new roads to Rochdale. Up and down platforms were provided here, with a small wooden station building on the down side. The Rishworth branch was worked as a single line for much of its life, the down line being treated as the running line, while the former up line was used as a storage siding for spare rolling stock. Rakes of empty coaches could be placed on the branch with a space of not less than 30 yards between each set of vehicles, while LMS working appendices specified that the handbrakes had to be securely padlocked. The former station building became a Scout hut following closure of the station in 1929.

Left: Copley

Having left Sowerby Bridge, trains cross the River Calder and soon reaches Milner Royd Junction, at which point the Halifax line diverges from the original Manchester & Leeds route to Normanton. The junction is controlled from an interesting signal box, which is probably the only surviving example of a cabin constructed by Messrs Yardley, Smith & Co. for the Lancashire & Yorkshire Railway during the period from 1878 to 1882. Milner Royd Junction is, in effect, the western point of a triangle – the west-to-east curve that continues south-eastwards to Greetland Junction being an avoiding line for through services that do not call intermediately at Halifax. Taking the west-to-north arm of the triangle, Leeds workings climb at 1 in 118 as they pass the site of a long-closed station at Copley, which was opened in 1855 and closed in July 1931.

Right: Dryclough Junction

After passing through the short Bankhouse Tunnel, the route curves northwards as it approaches Dryclough Junction, where the north-to-east arm of the triangle trails in from the right; the east curve is currently used by trains from Leeds to Huddersfield via Bradford, and by 'Grand Central' workings between Bradford, Halifax and London. The picture shows Fairburn Class 4MT 2-6-4T No. 42083 passing Dryclough Junction Signal Box. Dryclough Junction was the scene of a minor accident that took place on 5 February 2011 when the 5.55 a.m. Hedden Bridge to Leeds service, worked by Class 158 unit No. 158851, was derailed by fallen debris following the collapse of a retaining wall during a period of heavy rain. Fortunately, the train remained upright and there were no injuries.

Halifax

Halifax station (32¾ miles) was opened on 1 July 1844, the first station being a temporary wooden terminus as the end of a single-track branch from Greetland Junction. As mentioned in the historical section, this line was promoted by the West Riding Union Railway, which was closely linked to the Manchester & Leeds Railway and, as such, became an integral part of the Lancashire & Yorkshire system. The Halifax branch was extended north-eastwards to Low Moor on 7 August 1850, a new station being opened at Halifax, around a quarter of a mile to the north of the original. The 1850 station was replaced on 24 June 1855, when a permanent station with impressive classical buildings was brought into use.

The railway history of Halifax is made more complicated by the presence of the Great Northern Railway, which built or acquired a number of lines in Yorkshire, including the Halifax & Ovenden Railway and the Halifax High Level line, which were jointly owned by the GNR and L&YR companies. The Halifax & Ovenden line was opened for freight traffic in 1874, but the intervening section between Queensbury and Bradford presented considerable engineering difficulties, and passenger services did not commence until 1878–79. The Halifax High Level line was opened in 1890 and taken over by the L&YR and GNR companies in 1894.

Halifax station was extensively reconstructed during the 1880s, when separate platforms were provided for GNR services. The upper picture provides a general view of the station approach, while the lower view shows the platforms.

Opposite: Halifax

A detailed view of the station approach: the Lancashire & Yorkshire booking office is visible to the left of the picture, while the Great Northern booking office can be seen to the right.

Left: Halifax

A further view of the station during the early years of the twentieth century. The railway system in and around Halifax was severely rationalised during the British Railways period, the former Great Northern lines to the north and east of the town being closed to passengers with effect from 23 May 1955, while the main lines through Halifax were run down during the Beeching years. It would be no exaggeration to say that Halifax station is merely a shadow of its former self, the present rationalised facilities being entirely inappropriate in relation to a town of 82,000 inhabitants. Only two platforms remain in use and although the handsome station building has survived, it is no longer in railway use as this Grade II-listed Victorian building has become a museum and children's nursery. A modern, albeit much smaller building, incorporating a ticket office and waiting area, has been built to the north of the old station building, and this is linked to the remaining platforms by a fully enclosed footbridge.

Right: Halifax

Halifax East Signal Box was opened in 1884 to replace an earlier signal box. This typical Lancashire & Yorkshire box was a Railway Signal Co. standard design containing a seventy-lever frame, which was relocked with tappet locking around 1892. The box was renamed 'Halifax' on 30 March 1969, and the lever frame was replaced at around the same time.

Left: Halifax – Some Tickets

A selection of Edmondson card tickets from the central section of the Calder Valey route between Hebden Bridge, Halifax and Bradford Exchange. The return ticket from Hebden Bridge to Halifax (No. 9337) was one of the last Edmondson tickets issued by BR and, although still printed on an Edmonson card, the traditional print layout has been replaced by 'cash register'-style lettering. The third-class single from Bradford Exchange to Laisterdyke (No. 4249) was issued by the London & North Eastern Railway – Bradford Exchange having been a joint station which was shared by the L&YR and Great Northern companies.

Right: Lines Around Halifax – The Halifax & Ovenden Railway

A general view of Ovenden station, on the jointly owned Halifax & Ovenden Railway. The Halifax & Ovenden line was opened for the carriage of passengers on 15 December 1879, but Ovenden station was not opened until 2 June 1881. The Halifax & Ovenden line was worked by Great Northern (later LNER) locomotives and rolling stock, Ivatt N1 Class 0-6-2Ts being used on the route during the BR period. The branch was closed with effect from 23 May 1955; the platforms and station buildings were of timber-framed construction, as shown in this Edwardian postcard view.

GREETLAND.
L&Y.

Left: Lines Around Halifax – The Stainland Branch

In 1865, the L&YR obtained parliamentary consent for a short branch running southwards from the original Calder Valley main line at Greetland to the mill town of Stainland – a distance of 1¾ miles. However, the line was not opened until 1 January 1875: the progress of the scheme was impeded by the economic crisis that followed the failure of bankers Overend, Gurney & Co. in May 1866. The new line was double track throughout, with major viaducts at Stainland and West Vale. There were, for many years, around half-a-dozen trains each way, most of these services being through workings between Stainland and Halifax, which continued northwards via Greetland Junction and Dryclough Junction. In 1907, the L&YR introduced a steam railmotor service, and an additional stopping place was opened at Rochdale Road, between Greetland and West Vale. The photograph shows Greetland station around 1912.

Right: Lines Around Halifax – The Stainland Branch

The intermediate station at West Vale was opened with the line on 1 January 1875. Its track layout incorporated up and down platforms for passenger traffic, with a goods yard on the up side and a level crossing immediately to the north. The hip-roofed station buildings were of brick construction, with full-length canopies. The Halifax tramway system reached West Vale in 1905 and, thereafter, the railway suffered from tramway competition. In an attempt to attract more passengers, the Lancashire & Yorkshire Railway provided a lavish train service, with up to seventeen railmotor trips each way by 1910.

Opposite: Lines Around Halifax – The Stainland Branch

An Edwardian postcard view showing L&YR steam railmotor No. 3 at Stainland.

WEST VALE L&Y.

L&Y LIGHT MOTOR TRAIN
STAINLAND

Right: **Lines Around Halifax – The Stainland Branch**

Another view of the terminus at Stainland, showing the substantially built station building with its glazed platform canopy. The Lancashire & Yorkshire Railway seems to have been particularly proud of its steam railmotors, which feature in several of these Edwardian postcard views. The Lancashire & Yorkshire Railway introduced eighteen of these units at various times between 1906 and 1911, the L&YR railmotors being more successful than many of their contemporaries on other lines. Each unit consisted of a tiny locomotive and a single-passenger vehicle, the coach portion having just one bogie at the 'outer' end, as the 'inner' end of the vehicle was attached to the engine. The engines and coaches were interchangeable, which meant that, when the locomotive was in need of maintenance or repair, the coach was able to remain in operation.

Opposite: **Lines Around Halifax – The Stainland Branch**

Hughes railmotor No. 4 pauses at West Vale while working on the Stainland branch during the early 1900s.

Left: **Lines Around Halifax – The Stainland Branch**

The terminus at Stainland consisted of a single platform, the hipped-roof station building being in the same architectural 'family' as its counterpart at West Vale. When opened in 1875, the station was known simply as Stainland, but the name was changed to Stainland & Holywell Green in 1892. Despite the relatively full train service provided on the Halifax to Stainland branch, the railway was unable to compete with tramway competition, and the line was closed to passengers with effect from Monday 29 September 1929, although goods traffic was carried for another three decades.

WEST VALE STATION AND MOTOR

Hipperholme

Having left Halifax, present-day trains proceed north-eastwards on a gently rising gradient of 1 in 235, which continues through the 1,105 yard Beacon Hill Tunnel before steepening slightly to 1 in 200. The now-closed station at Hipperholme (34¼ miles) was opened by the Lancashire & Yorkshire Railway on 7 August 1850 and closed with effect from 8 June 1953 – though facilities remained in use for occasional excursion traffic, and freight was handled until 1966. The station was situated in a cutting spanned by a plate girder bridge, while the up and down platforms were linked by a plate girder footbridge. The main station building was a substantial, two-storey structure incorporating a street-level booking office and additional buildings on the platform. Further accommodation for waiting travellers was provided in a subsidiary building on the opposite platform.

Opposite: Hipperholme

A further view of Hipperholme station, showing the high-level booking office and the low-level platform buildings.

LANCASHIRE & YORKSHIRE RAILWAY.
BOOKING OFFICE.

HIPPERHOLME

HIPPERHOLME STATION 174

Lightcliffe

Still climbing at 1 in 200, trains pass through a short tunnel before reaching the site of another closed stopping place at Lightcliffe (35 miles), less than 1 mile further on. Opened on 7 August 1850, Lightcliffe was equipped with slightly staggered platforms, the up and down sides being linked by a lattice girder footbridge. The main station building was a Tudor-style structure, incorporating a single-storey waiting room portion and a two-storey stationmaster's house – the domestic portion being to the right (when viewed from the platform). The goods contained a range of accommodation for coal, livestock, horseboxes, road vehicles and general merchandise, while a 10-ton yard was available for large or heavy consignments. The photographs show the station during the early years of the twentieth century.

Lightcliffe station was closed with effect from Monday 14 June 1965, on which day the North Eastern Region of British Railways withdrew passenger services between Bradford Exchange and Huddersfield via Halifax and via Mirfield, resulting in the closure of six local stations.

Opposite: Lightcliffe

A final view of Lightcliffe station, as depicted in an Edwardian photograph dating from around 1909.

Left: Wyke & Norwood Green

Wyke & Norwood Green (36¼ miles), a little over 1 mile further on, was opened by the L&YR on 7 August 1850. This wayside stopping place was originally known as Pickle Bridge, but its name was changed to Wyke in 1882, before the name Wyke & Norwood Green was finally adopted. The station was moved to a new site in 1896, the new station being around 13 chains to the east of the original. The photograph, dating from around 1912, is looking east towards Leeds, the west portal of Wyke Tunnel being visible in the distance; this tunnel has a length of 1,365 yards. The station was formerly the junction for the Pickle Bridge branch, which had originally been promoted in the 1840s as part of the West Riding Union scheme, but was not opened until 1881. This 3¾-mile branch was closed in 1948, and Wyke & Norwood Green station was closed with effect from 21 September 1953.

Right: Low Moor

Heading north-eastwards on a rising gradient of 1 in 290, trains soon reach the site of Low Moor station (38 miles), which was opened on 18 July 1848 and closed with effect from 14 June 1965. In operational terms, Low Moor was a place of considerable importance, insofar as it was the junction for the Bradford Exchange line, and the point at which the Bradford portions of Manchester to Leeds expresses were attached or detached from the Leeds portions, which avoided Bradford by taking the Laisterdyke to Bowling line. The infrastructure here was quite extensive, as shown in the accompanying view of the station during the early years of the twentieth century. The main station building, visible to the left, contained a range of accommodation, including a booking office, parcels office, toilets for both sexes and separate waiting rooms for first- and third-class travellers.

Opposite: Low Moor

A general view of Low Moor station during the early 1900s.

Right: Bradford Exchange

On leaving Low Moor, trains head northwards on a rising gradient of 1 in 263 before plunging into the 1,648 yard Bowling Tunnel on a falling gradient of 1 in 420, which steepens to 1 in 50 for the final descent into Bradford (39¾ miles). Bradford was first served by rail on 1 July 1846, when the Midland Railway opened a terminus at Market Street. The Lancashire & Yorkshire station at Drake Street was opened a little over four years later on 9 May 1850, while the Great Northern Railway reached Bradford on 1 August 1854, the first GNR terminus being sited at Aldophus Street, around 1 mile from the city centre. On 7 January 1867, the Great Northern route was extended westwards to Drake Street and the earlier station at Adolphus Street was, thereafter, relegated to the status of a goods depot. In connection with this scheme, Drake Street station was enlarged, and its name was changed to Bradford Exchange. The rebuilt station was wholly owned by the L&YR, but the Great Northern shared the station as tenants.

Left: Low Moor

In addition to its role as the junction for Bradford, Low Moor was also the junction for the Spen Valley line to Mirfield and the site of a motive power depot. The Spen Valley line was authorised as part of the West Riding Union scheme and ceremonially opened on Wednesday 12 July 1848. Regular services commenced on Tuesday 18 July, and the line remained in operation for passenger traffic until June 1965. Freight lasted for a few more years – the final traffic being in connection with an oil terminal at Liversedge. Low Moor shed was opened under L&YR auspices in 1866 and enlarged in 1889, while new coaling and ash plants were installed during the LMS era. The shed building was a six-road structure, while the usual allocation was around thirty-five locomotives. In 1959, Low Moor received an influx of B1 Class 4-6-0s, J50 0-6-0Ts and other ex-LNER locomotive classes following the closure of Bradford (Hammerton Street) shed, and this caused the allocation to be increased to seventy engines.

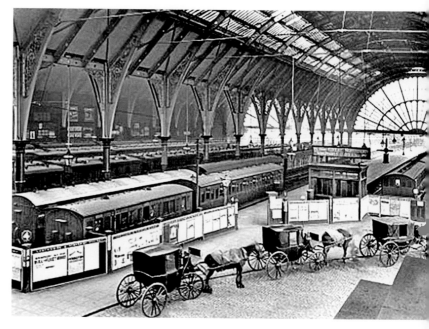

Left: Bradford Forster Square

A glimpse of the Midland terminus at Bradford Market Street, which was sited to the north of Bradford Exchange. Market Street was replaced by a new six-platform station on 2 March 1890 and, in 1924, the Midland terminus was renamed Bradford Forster Square. Plans were put forward at various times for a connecting line between the Midland and L&YR systems, one of these schemes being the aptly named Bradford Central Railway, which would have left the Midland at Queen's Road bridge and passed to the west of Market Street in order to join the L&YR at Drake Street. The proposed line would have been around 1¼ miles in length and it would have incorporated a new 'Central Station' serving all of the railways in Bradford. Plans were submitted to Parliament for the 1884 session, but in the event nothing came of the proposal and the local railway system has remained fragmented and inconvenient, with two separate terminal stations – neither of which are of main-line character.

Right: Bradford Exchange

Stanier Black Five 4-6-0 No. 44983 departs from Bradford Exchange with an express passenger working during the mid-1950s. The distinctive twin-span overall roof that can be seen in the background consisted of two 100-ft train sheds, supported by side walls and eighteen centrally placed cast-iron columns. Its overall dimensions were 450 feet by 200 feet and it covered most of the platforms. Sadly, this impressive structure was torn down during the 1970s because Bradford Exchange station was considered to be 'too large for present requirements'. A new, much smaller, station was opened on Monday 14 January 1973, this new facility being part of a combined bus and rail station which was itself redeveloped in 1999. The present-day station, known as Bradford Interchange, has four terminal platforms that are covered by canopies for much of their length, while run-round facilities enable the station to deal with locomotive-hauled workings.

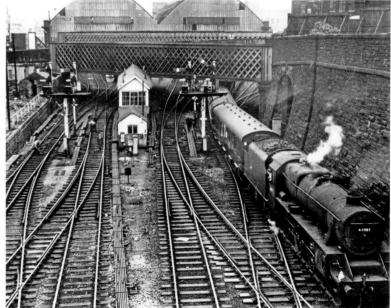

THE YORKSHIRE PULLMAN
(Limited Train)

WEEKDAYS
(Bank Holidays excepted)

		S pm	E pm				E am	S am
London (King's Cross)	dep	5 8	5 30	Harrogate	dep	10 7		10 37
Doncaster	arr	8 7	8 14	Bradford (Exchange)	,,	10 15		10 47
Goole	,,	8 41	8 48	Leeds (Central)	,,	10 45		11 17
Hull	,,	9 15	9 21	Wakefield (Westgate)	,,	11 5		11 37
Wakefield (Westgate)	,,	8 38	8 44	Hull	,,	10 30		11 0
Leeds (Central).. ..	,,	9 0	9 5	Goole	,,	11 0		11 30
Bradford (Exchange)	,,	9 26	9 31					
				Doncaster	,,	11 40		12 10
Harrogate	,,	9 40	9 45				pm	
				London (King's Cross)	arr	2 30		3 8

E—Except Saturdays.   S—Saturdays only.

MEALS AND REFRESHMENTS SERVED AT EVERY SEAT
SUPPLEMENTARY FARES (For each Single Journey)
Children under 14 years of age half price

THE SOUTH YORKSHIREMAN

BRADFORD, HUDDERSFIELD, SHEFFIELD,
NOTTINGHAM, LEICESTER,
LONDON (Marylebone)

WEEKDAYS

		am				pm
Bradford (Exchange)	dep	10 0	London (Marylebone)	dep	4 50
Halifax Town	,,	10 16	Aylesbury (Town)	,,	5 48
Brighouse	,,	10 28			
Huddersfield	,,	10 43	Leicester (Central)	arr	7 0
Sheffield (Victoria)	,,	11 34	Nottingham (Victoria)	,,	7 32
		pm	Sheffield (Victoria)	,,	8 37
Nottingham (Victoria)	,,	12 35	Penistone	,,	9 6
Loughborough (Central)	,,	12 54	Huddersfield	,,	9 32
Leicester (Central)	,,	1 11	Brighouse	,,	9 46
Rugby (Central)..	,,	1 39	Halifax Town	,,	10 0
Aylesbury (Town)	arr	2 35	Bradford (Exchange).. ..	,,	10 17
London (Marylebone)	,,	3 29			

Refreshment Cars available between Sheffield (Victoria) and London (Marylebone).

Passengers travelling from Bradford (Exchange), Halifax Town, Huddersfield,
Sheffield (Victoria) and London (Marylebone) by these services can reserve seats in advance
on payment of a fee of 1s. 0d. per seat.

Bradford – *The Yorkshire Pullman* & *The South Yorkshireman*

In steam days, Bradford Exchange was regarded very much as a 'main line' station, its 'InterCity' status being underlined by the provision of a number of daily named trains, including *The Yorkshire Pullman*, *The South Yorkshireman*, *The West Riding* and *The White Rose*. The prestigious *Yorkshire Pullman* was introduced by the LNER in 1925 and revived by BR in 1946, while the *The South Yorkshireman* was introduced in 1946 as a through service between Bradford and London Marylebone, via the Great Central route.

These two timebills show the timings of *The Yorkshire Pullman* and *The South Yorkshireman* in 1956. In the up direction, *The Yorkshire Pullman* started its journey at Harrogate at 10.07 a.m. and left Bradford Exchange at 10.15 a.m., arriving at King's Cross by 2.30 p.m. In the down direction, the northbound working was scheduled to leave Kings Cross at 5.30 p.m., reaching Bradford at 9.31 p.m. and Harrogate at 9.45 p.m. The usual formation on leaving London was eleven Pullman cars, including portions for Leeds, Bradford and Hull.

The South Yorkshireman left Bradford Exchange at 10.00 a.m. and returned from Marylebone at 4.50 p.m., calling intermediately at Halifax, Huddersfield, Sheffield, Nottingham Victoria, Leicester Central, Rugby Central and Aylesbury. The train was withdrawn in 1960, although in recent years a train with the same name has been introduced on the Midland main line between Sheffield and London St Pancras. Bradford to London through trains reappeared in 2010 in the form of 'Grand Central' services to and from Kings Cross via Pontefract and Doncaster.

Left: Bradford – Some Tickets

A selection of BR tickets issued from stations between Bradford Exchange and Leeds. The examples shown here include paper platform tickets from Bradford Forster Square and Bradford Exchange, and Edmondson card tickets from Bramley, Laisterdyke and Leeds.

Right: St Dunstan's

Bradford Exchange is, in effect, at the end of a branch and a reversal is necessary before eastbound workings can resume their journeys over the final 9½ miles of the route to Leeds. This easternmost section of the route had originally been planned as part of the West Riding Union Railway, but the L&YR allowed the scheme to lapse and a new Great Northern-backed company known as The Leeds, Bradford & Halifax Junction Railway was authorised in 1852, in order to complete missing link between Bowling and Leeds. The Leeds to Bradford line was opened on 1 August 1854, the L&YR having running powers into Leeds, while the GNR had reciprocal powers over the Lancashire & Yorkshire system from Bowling to Halifax and Bradford. There are three closed stations at the Bradford end of the GNR line – St Dunstan's having lost its passenger services in September 1952, while Bowling Junction was closed in February 1951 and neighbouring Bowling Junction was closed as long ago as 1895.

Left: **Laisterdyke**

The eastern exit from Bradford Exchange includes 2 miles of steeply rising gradients, mainly at 1 in 50–58, which ease to 1 in 100 on the approach to Laisterdyke. This station was opened by the GNR on 1 August 1854 and closed with effect from 4 July 1966. The infrastructure at Laisterdyke incorporated twin island platforms with extensive buildings on both sides, together with a street-level station building and a fully enclosed footbridge. A triangular junction to the east of the passenger station gave access to the GNR route from Wakefield to Shipley, entry to the triangle being controlled from Laisterdyke East Signal Box, which was fitted with a seventy-five-lever Saxby & Farmer frame. In pre-Grouping days, the GNR operated around 115 miles of passenger line in this part of Yorkshire, but 75 miles of line had been closed by 1966 – one of the victims being the Laisterdyke to Shipley route, which lost its passenger services in 1931.

Right: **Bramley**

Heading south-eastwards, the Leeds route passes beneath the long-closed GNR branch to Shipley and, descending at 1 in 100, trains then glide through the 455-yard Hillfoot Tunnel (also known as Stanningley Tunnel) before coming to rest at New Pudsey. Opened on 6 March 1967, New Pudsey was initially seen as a local replacement for the Pudsey branch (closed in 1964), but it soon became popular as a Park and Ride station and, as such, it now serves as a railhead for the surrounding area. From New Pudsey the route continues its descent through the abandoned station at Stanningley (closed 1968) to Bramley. This station was opened by the Great Northern Railway on 1 August 1854, and closed with effect from 4 July 1966. However, reopening took place on 12 September 1983, and Bramley now generates around 0.3 million passenger journeys per annum. The photograph shows the station approach during the early 1900s.

Opposite: **Laisterdyke**

Stanier Class 5MT 4-6-0 No. 44693 heads a passenger working through Laisterdyke during the BR period.

GREAT NORTHERN RAILWAY
to BRAMLEY STATION

Left: Bramley

A postcard view of Bramley during the Edwardian period; the ornate station building can be seen in the distance. The present-day Bramley station is an unstaffed stopping place with staggered up and down platforms and glazed waiting shelters on each side. Bramley was formerly the junction for the Pudsey branch (or the 'Pudsey Loop', as it was sometimes called), which formed an alternative route between Bramley, Pudsey and Laisterdyke. The first regular diesel multiple-unit service in the north was introduced between Leeds Central, Harrogate and Bradford in 1954, most of the Leeds trains being routed via the main line while others used the Pudsey Loop. Sadly, traffic was on the decline and the service was withdrawn with effect from 15 June 1964, the Pudsey Loop being closed in its entirety a few weeks later.

Right: Armley Moor

Armley Moor station, on the western outskirts of Leeds, was opened with the line on 1 August 1854 and closed with effect from 4 July 1966; it was known as Armley & Wortley until 1950. The photograph provides a detailed view of the ornate, Tudor-Gothic-style station building that incorporated domestic accommodation for the stationmaster and his family. As they approach Leeds, trains reach Whitehall Junction and the Whitehall Curve, which was realigned in 1967 so that Calder Valley services to and from the modernised Leeds City station could be accessed.

Opposite: Bramley

An Edwardian postcard view showing the station approach during the early 1900s. The Tudor-Gothic-style station building was clearly in the same architectural 'family' as its counterpart at Armley.

Leeds

At the time of the Grouping in 1923, the Leeds was served by three main-line stations, Wellington having been developed as the principal Midland Railway terminus, while the adjacent 'Leeds New' station (opened in 1869) was shared between the London & North Western and North Eastern railways. A third station, known as 'Leeds Central', was used by the Great Northern, Lancashire & Yorkshire Railway, North Eastern, London & North Western and Great Central companies. Wellington and Leeds New stations were combined to form Leeds City Station on 2 May 1938, although the nearby Leeds Central station was unaffected by the change. The photographs provide a glimpse of Leeds New station during the early 1900s.

A major reconstruction scheme was put into effect in the 1960s, when British Railways decided to eliminate Leeds Central and concentrate all passenger services in Leeds City station, the much-enlarged City station being officially opened on 17 May 1967. In its new form, the station had twelve passenger platforms and additional platforms for parcels traffic. The platforms were linked by a subway and a footbridge, while an overhead 'barrow way' or parcels bridge was provided at the west end of the station. The whole complex was dominated by ugly multistorey office buildings, some of which had been designed by the criminal architect John Poulson (1910–93). The spacious North Concourse, which had been opened in 1938, was retained but access to the platforms was from a new South Concourse, with its main entrance in New Street.

Opposite: Leeds

A further postcard view of Leeds New station during the Edwardian period. A Midland train can be seen to the right.

Right: Leeds

A platform view at the modernised Leeds City station, taken by Roger Suttcliffe on 13 February 1987. Class 45 locomotive No. 45144 can be seen to the left, while an HST set headed by power car No. 43193 waits in the adjacent platform.

Left: Leeds

A further reconstruction scheme was carried out between 1999 and 2002 and, as a result, the 1960s canopies were replaced by a new glass roof and the North Concourse was refurbished, allowing travellers to admire its 1930s-style art deco features. The present-day station has six through platforms and eleven terminal bays; new platforms were added on the south side, while the former parcels platforms on the north side of the station have been reopened for passengers. Many of the platforms are subdivided into up to four sections, making a grand total of no less than forty-seven platforms. This large and complex station now handles over 27 million passengers per annum, making it one of the busiest stations in the country. The photograph shows Class 141 railbus No. 141004 at the east end of the station in 1984.

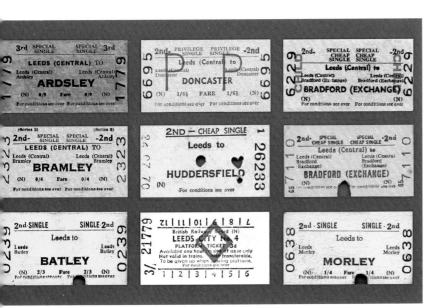

Left: Leeds – Some Tickets

A selection of British Railways tickets issued at Leeds, comprising a paper platform ticket, seven Edmondson card tickets and a machine-issued paper travel ticket. First-class tickets were normally white, whereas LMS and BR second- and third-class issues were printed on light-greenish-grey cards. The mauve tickets were cheap singles. Five of the tickets were issued at Leeds Central, which closed in 1967 with its services being diverted into the nearby Leeds City station.

Right: **Leeds**
Stanier Jubilee Class 4-6-0 No. 45573 *Newfoundland* is seen at Leeds Holbeck shed in 1965. Holbeck was a standard Midland Railway 'square' roundhouse, with two internal turntables, each of which fed a number of radial sidings.

Right: Leeds

Fowler Class 4MT 2-6-4T No. 42394 at Holbeck shed around 1965.

Left: Leeds

A glimpse of the former Great Northern Railway shed at Leeds Copley Hill, with a range of GNR locomotives on view. This five-road shed was opened in 1900 and closed in 1964.

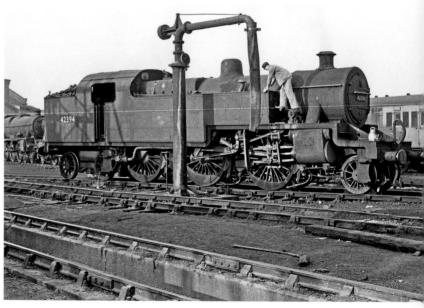

Left: **Hall Royd Junction & The Copy Pit Route**

Having examined the stations and other infrastructure on the Calder Valley route between Manchester Victoria and Leeds, we must now return westwards in order to explore the Copy Pit line from Hall Royd Junction to Burnley and Blackburn. As mentioned earlier, this former Lancashire & Yorkshire route narrowly escaped closure during the early 1980s, but there has been a welcome revival in recent years and the line now carries regular passenger services between Burnley and Manchester, together with longer distance trans-Pennine workings and significant amounts of freight traffic. The photograph shows Class 158 unit No. 158796 *Fred Trueman – Cricketing Legend* taking the Copy Pit route at Hall Royd Junction while working the late-running 8.27 a.m. York to Blackpool North Northern service on 16 November 2015. The 225-yard Millwood Tunnel can be seen in the background.

Right: **Hall Royd Junction & The Copy Pit Route**
Class 158 unit No. 158756 heads west towards Sowerby Bridge with the 8.51 a.m. Leeds to Manchester working on 16 November 2015.

Cornholme

Heading north-west from the Todmorden Triangle, Copy Pit services follow the narrow Calder Valley passing, en route, the site of an abandoned stopping place at Stansfield Hall which was opened around 1871 and closed in July 1944. Maintaining its north-westerly heading, the railway then runs through Lydgate Tunnel before trains reach the site of Cornholme station, which was opened by the L&YR in 1878 and closed in September 1938.

Cornholme was the scene of an accident on the night of 15 August 1967, when a freight train headed by Class 40 diesel locomotive No. D398 ran into a Class 8F 2-8-0 after the driver of the diesel locomotive, who had recently consumed 'the equivalent of five or six pints of beer', ignored all speed limits on the 1 in 80 descent from Copy Pit Summit and ran past six danger signals. The driver (who had presumably fallen asleep at the controls) received fatal injuries and the freight train was derailed; one of its wagons ended up in the kitchen of a nearby house, while others landed in back gardens.

The upper picture provides a panoramic view of Cornholme during the early years of the twentieth century, Cornholme station being visible to the left of the factory chimney. The lower picture shows Class 158 unit No. 158848 heading eastwards along the Calder Valley at Cornholme with the 10.11 a.m. Blackpool North to York Northern Rail service on 16 March 2015.

Opposite: Cornholme

Northern Rail Class 158 unit No. 158752 passes Cornholme while working the 10.27 a.m. York to Blackpool North service on 16 March 2015. Frostholme Mill, now the home of the Sutcliffe Furniture Co., dominates the centre of the picture, while St Michael's Church can be seen in the background.

Portsmouth

Left: Continuing their 1 in 80 ascent along the Calder Valley, westbound services pass through the closed station at Portsmouth, which was opened with the line on 12 November 1849 and lost its passenger services in July 1958.

Below left: A postcard view of the station, dating from the early years of the twentieth century. The station buildings here were of timber-framed construction with hipped roofs and horizontal weatherboarding.

Below right: An unidentified Aspinall 2-4-2T tank engine pauses at Portsmouth.

Holme

Holme, formerly the next stopping place, was one of three intermediate stations opened with the line on 12 November 1849. It served the nearby village of Holme Chapel and, if contemporary press reports are to be believed, the station was originally known as Holmes Chapel. However, the name was shortened to Holme at an early date, presumably to prevent confusion with Holmes Chapel on the London & North Western Railway. The up and down platforms were equipped with wooden station buildings, as shown in the accompanying photographs, which date from the early twentieth century. Holme was closed by the LMS in July 1930, but private siding traffic continued to be dealt with at the nearby Cliviger and Copy Pit sidings.

Left: Holme

This interesting old photograph shows Holme station during the late Victorian period. The somewhat primitive wooden buildings were probably part of the original infrastructure – the more substantial, timber-framed structures that appear in the previous photographs being later additions. The locomotive appears to be a Yates 4 Class 2-4-0.

Right: Towneley

From Holme, the route continues to Towneley, the site of another defunct stopping place, which was opened on 12 November 1849 and closed in August 1952. As mentioned in the historical section, Towneley was initially known as Organ Row. As far as can be ascertained, Organ Row was a row of cottages in the Burnley Wood district of Burnley and, as such, it seems an odd choice of name for a railway station. Copy Pit Summit, near Towneley, derives its name from nearby coal workings. The photograph is a winter scene at Towneley during the early 1900s, showing the up and down platforms, signal cabin and level crossing.

Opposite: Holme

Class 33 locomotives Nos 33116 *Hertfordshire Railtours* and 33051 *Shakespeare Cliff* slog up the gradient towards Copy Pit Summit on 28 December 1996 with the 7.55 a.m. Hertfordshire Railtours 'Duck & Weasel' railtour from Kings Cross to York. The train is passing Holme Chapel, while Burnley is just about visible through the mist in the background.

Left: Towneley

A postcard view of Towneley station during the early 1900s, showing the platforms, signal cabin and level crossing, together with the station building, which contained domestic accommodation for the stationmaster and his family. A party of schoolchildren have been assembled on the crossing – perhaps at the start of a Sunday school outing?

Right: Towneley

An unidentified L&YR 4-4-0 locomotive is pictured at Towneley with a four-coach passenger train. The station building seems to have been obscured by steam. Towneley station was closed with effect from 4 August 1952, but the station building survived as a private dwelling, while the signal cabin was retained as a gate box. As such, this gable-roofed structure remains in use at the time of writing, although it is likely to be abolished in the near future.

Opposite: Copy Pit Summit

Class 31 locomotives Nos 31554 and 31112 surmount Copy Pit Summit in the rain while hauling the 7.24 a.m. Pathfinder Tours Bristol Temple Meads to Doncaster 'Yorkshire Doodle Dandy' railtour on 13 July 1996. Copy Pit, some 849 (749?) feet above mean sea level, derives its name from nearby coal workings.

BURNLEY CTL. L▸▸▸

Burnley – Manchester Road & Burnley Central

Having surmounted Copy Pit summit, trains descend towards Burnley, 39¼ miles from Leeds. When it opened on 12 November 1849, the line from Todmorden had terminated in a small station at Thorneybank but this was replaced by an improved station on the opposite side of Manchester Road on 1 November 1866. Burnley Manchester Road was closed to passengers with effect from 6 November 1961, although freight traffic was handled until October 1972. However, this was not the end of the story, and the station was reopened on 13 October 1986 as part of the revival of the Copy Pit line. This was, in fact, two weeks later than scheduled, a 'mystery geological fault' having caused the hillsides around Holme Tunnel to move around 4 inches, necessitating the provision of 'a steel ribcage' within the tunnel to prevent further movement.

The new station, which cost £127,000 and was paid for by Lancashire County Council, consisted of up and down platforms with simple waiting shelters but, following a recent upgrading programme (at a cost of £2.3 million) Burnley Manchester Road has acquired an impressive new station building, additional car-parking spaces and improved waiting shelters, while traffic has been increasing steadily for several years – around 0.25 million passenger journeys are generated each year. The line continues westwards from Burnley Manchester Road to Gannow Junction, at which point the Copy Pit route converges with the East Lancashire line from Preston to Colne.

The former East Lancashire station at Burnley was opened on 1 December 1848, and it was, for many years, regarded as Burnley's principal station. The station was originally known simply as Burnley, but the name 'Burnley Bank Top' was adopted in 1871 and in 1944 it became Burnley Central. Freight-handling facilities were withdrawn in August 1970 and the goods yard has disappeared, while a public park on the right-hand side of the line now occupies the site of sidings used in conjunction with a local colliery. The upper photograph shows the old station prior to reconstruction, while the lower view shows a steam railmotor and a 2-4-2T in the station around 1910.

Left: The Colne Line – Briarfield

The Colne route was reduced to a single track between Gannow Junction and Chaffers Siding in 1986, resulting in considerable rationalisation at Burnley Central and the closure of Burnley Central signal box. Burnley Central station is now a single-platform stopping place with a modern station building on the former up platform. The now singled line continues north-eastwards from Burnley, passing through Brierfield and Nelson on its way to Colne. The photograph provides a general view of Brierfield station, on the now truncated section of line between Burnley and Colne, showing the platforms, station buildings, signal cabin and level crossing; an Aspinall 2-4-2T stands in the station with a passenger working.

Right: The Colne Line – Colne

An Edwardian postcard view of Colne station which, since the closure of the former Midland route to Skipton in 1970, is the end of a lengthy 28¾-mile branch from Preston. Only one platform remains in use, and the station building has been replaced by a simple 'bus stop'-style waiting shelter. An unidentified Midland Railway 2-4-0 can be seen to the right of the picture. Present-day train services run between Blackpool and Colne at hourly intervals, with a train every two hours on Sundays.

Right: Burnley Barracks

Burnley Barracks, the next stopping place, was first served by rail on 18 September 1848, when the East Lancashire Railway was opened to a temporary terminus at Burnley Barracks. This station, which derived its name from the adjacent army barracks, was primarily a passenger-only stopping place, although goods traffic was handled at the nearby Burnley Barracks Mineral Siding, which also dealt with private traffic for the Anglo-American Oil Co. On a footnote, it has been suggested that the station was originally called 'Burnley', but in its opening report in September 1848 *The Blackburn Standard* refers to it as 'the Burnley Barrack station'.

Left: The Colne Line – Colne

The rare sight of a locomotive-hauled train on the Colne branch, as Class 26 locomotives Nos 26003 and 26005 pass Reedley to the north of Burnley, with the 1.40 p.m. Pathfinder Tours Preston to Preston (via Padiham and Colne) 'Lancastrian Mini Excursion' on 23 May 1993. Class 60 locomotive No. 60084 is out of sight at the rear of the train – engines being required at each end of the train as there are no longer any run-round facilities at Colne. This excursion was one of a number of mini railtours organised by Pathfinder over the weekend using (by today's standards) an amazing variety of traction.

Rose Grove

Rose Grove, just 1 mile beyond Burnley Barracks and 40¾ miles from Leeds, was opened by the East Lancashire Railway on 18 September 1848. In steam days, the infrastructure at Rose Grove incorporated a spacious island platform with bays at each end, while much of the platform was covered by a glass and iron canopy. The station was rebuilt and 'improved' in 1970, when BR removed the platform canopy and installed electric lighting in place of the earlier gas lamps. The present-day station, now an unstaffed halt, is merely a shadow of its former self, the station buildings having been replaced by a simple shelter, while the bays that formerly existed at each end of the single-island platform have been filled in. A programme of improvements has recently been carried out, and the station has now acquired a new waiting shelter, a customer information screen, CCTV cameras and a ticket vending machine.

For steam enthusiasts, Rose Grove will be remembered as the site of an important motive power depot, which was coded 24B from 1948 until 1963, and 10F thereafter. The shed building was a six-road structure with a ridge-and-furrow roof, while the usual offices, mess rooms, coaling and watering facilities were provided, together with an engine turntable. In BR days, the usual allocation comprised about fifty locomotives, including Black Five 4-6-0s, Crab 2-6-0s, Stanier Class 8F 2-8-0s, WD 2-8-0s, Class 4MT 2-6-4Ts, and Class 3F 0-6-0T shunting locomotives.

The upper photograph shows the original station building at Rose Grove; this small structure was in the Italianate style with a covered loggia, or waiting area, at the front of the building. The lower view shows the island platform around 1912.

Rose Grove

Left above: Class 60 locomotive No. 60084 *Cross Fell* passes Rose Grove station with the 1.40 p.m. Pathfinder Tours Preston to Preston (via Padiham and Colne) 'Lancastrian Mini Excursion' railtour on 23 May 1993. Class 26 locomotives Nos 26003 and 26005 can just be seen at the rear of the train (*see page 119*). Rose Grove will forever be associated with the dying days of steam operation on BR in 1968. There was a huge railway presence at this location: the derelict-looking wasteland, seen to the right of this picture, being occupied by sidings, while Rose Grove Motive Power depot covered most of the area now occupied by the M65 motorway, which can be seen in the background.

Left below: This final view of Rose Grove, during the early years of the twentieth century, shows details of the station building and the underside of the platform canopy. From Rose Grove, the route heads due west to Hapton (43¼ miles), where the station has gained welcome extra traffic from neighbouring housing developments. Climbing a series of rising gradients, the route reaches a miniature summit near Huncoat station (43¾ miles). Opened on 18 September 1848, Huncoat is a wayside stopping place with up and down platforms and a lattice girder footbridge. Enfield Road crosses the line on the level immediately to the west of the platforms – a typical L&YR gable-roofed signal cabin being retained as a gate box. The 1938 Railway Clearing House *Handbook of Stations* reveals that the, now closed, goods yard could handle coal class traffic and general merchandise, while private sidings served the Accrington Brick & Tile Co., Huncoat Colliery and other local industries, the colliery sidings being on the down side of the line.

Opposite: Rose Grove

A panoramic photograph of Rose Grove motive power depot, taken from the top of the coaling plant during the mid-1960s, and showing a number of Stanier Class 8F 2-8-0 freight locomotives, including Nos 48327, 48666 and 48727.

Accrington

As westbound trains approach Accrington (45½ miles), they are carried high above the town on a huge viaduct with twenty-one semicircular masonry arches, each with a span of 40 ft. The viaduct is built on a 40-chain curve and its arches are of brick construction with stone piers, stone facings and rusticated stone voussoirs. Three skew spans that cross the Whalley Road at the north end of the viaduct are separated from the main structure by a short length of embankment.

Accrington occupied a nodal position in the East Lancashire network, being the point at which the Blackburn, Burnley, Colne & Accrington Extension Railway converged with the line from Preston, In steam days, the station boasted a triangular layout, but in recent years all trains have used the sharply curved Colne line platforms. Accrington engine shed (24A) housed around thirty locomotives during the British Railways period, including Black Five 4-6-0s, WD 2-8-0s, Class 5MT 2-6-0s, Class 4MT 2-6-4Ts and Class 3F 0-6-0Ts. The shed was closed to steam in 1961, but it remained in use as a diesel multiple-unit depot.

In January 1970, *The Railway Magazine* reported that a new booking office was being built on the down platform, but the buildings on the up side were to be demolished when East Lancashire parcels traffic was transferred to a new 'concentration point'. Further changes were put into effect in 2011, when the station underwent a £2-million rebuild as part of a project to create 'a model of sustainable energy use for a railway station'. The 1970s ticket office was replaced by a new building that incorporated 'a rainwater harvesting system, photovoltaic cells and solar hot water generation panels'.

Right: Church & Oswaldtwistle

A postcard view of Church & Oswaldtwistle station from around 1912, showing the rear elevation of the main station building. Note the single-line electric tramway passing beneath the railway bridge.

Left: Church & Oswaldtwistle

Leaving Accrington, trains run westwards on a gently falling gradient for a little under 1 mile to Church & Oswaldtwistle (46¼ miles). Interestingly, Church grew up around a calico-printing works which was owned by the Peel family and, by the mid-nineteenth century, this part of Lancashire had developed into a specialised fabric printing and chemical centre. The station, which opened on 19 June 1848, was originally known as Church, but its name was changed to Church & Oswaldtwistle in 1895. Its up and down platforms are linked by an underline subway and the substantial station buildings that can be seen in the photographs have been replaced by glazed waiting shelters.

Right: **Rishton**
A further view of Rishton station, dating from the early twentieth century. The station has remained in operation, albeit as an unstaffed halt with round-topped waiting shelters in place of the Victorian station buildings. In recent years, the station has generated around 57,000 passenger journeys per year.

Opposite: **Rishton**
An Aspinall 2-4-2T pauses at Rishton with a three-coach passenger train.

Left: Rishton
Heading westwards, the line climbs at 1 in 132 as it approaches Rishton, a small mill town that grew up in the nineteenth century around textile factories owned by the Petre family of nearby Dunkenhalgh. The station, which opened with the line on 19 June 1848, features slightly staggered up and down platforms that are linked by a lattice girder footbridge. The main station building, now demolished, was a two-storey H-plan structure with two gabled cross wings, while the goods yard boasted a large gable-roofed goods shed, as shown in the photographs. The footbridge was formerly protected by a roof, but this has since been removed.

RISHTON STATION

Left: 'The North Lancashire Loop Line' – Padiham

As mentioned in the historical section, the now closed North Lancashire Loop Line formed an alternative route for passenger and freight traffic between Rose Grove and Great Harwood Junction, near Blackburn. The easternmost section between Rose Grove and Padiham was opened on 1 September 1876, and the line was completed throughout to Great Harwood Junction on Monday 15 October 1877. There were intermediate stations at Simonstone and Great Harwood, in addition to Padiham, which is shown here around 1912 with an Aspinall 2-4-2T beside the main station building.

Right: 'The North Lancashire Loop Line' – Padiham

An additional view of Padiham station during the halcyon years of the L&YR system before the First World War. The locomotive is another one of the ubiquitous L&YR radial 2-4-2Ts. No less than 330 of these engines were built between 1889 and 1911, some of the later examples having elongated bunkers. Many of these characteristic Lancashire & Yorkshire locomotives were scrapped in LMS days, but 123 survived long enough to become British Railways engines in 1948.

'The North Lancashire Loop'

Right: A detailed study of the hip-roofed station building at Simonstone, which featured a full-length platform canopy.

Below left: An Edwardian lady poses for the camera as a Lancashire & Yorkshire Railway 0-6-0 tender locomotive pauses on the bridge.

Below right: Great Harwood station building was very similar to that at nearby Simonstone. From Great Harwood, the loop line ran south-westwards to Great Harwood Junction, where it rejoined the main line. The North Lancashire Loop Line lost its passenger services with effect from 2 December 1957.

Railway Station, Blackburn.

Left: Blackburn

Entering the outskirts of Blackburn, trains reach Daisyfield Junction, where the line from Clitheroe and Hellifield converges from the right. Daisyfield station (which had platforms on the Hellifield line, but not on the Accrington route) was closed in November 1958. The line then passes through a short tunnel before trains draw to a halt at Blackburn station, 51¾ miles from Leeds. Opened on 1 June 1846, Blackburn remains an important traffic centre, being served by trains from Leeds, Colne, Preston, Manchester and Bolton. The station's lofty overall roof was demolished in 2000, by which time all traffic had been concentrated in the northernmost of the two island platforms, but the Grade II-listed station building, and a surprising amount of infrastructure, remains in place. Platform 4, on the south side of the station, was brought back into use in 2000, and in 2011 it was provided with a new platform canopy and a heated waiting room.

Right: Blackburn

Class 31 locomotives Nos 31410 *Granada Telethon* and the unnamed sister locomotive No. 31439 pull away from Blackburn station with the 7.15 p.m. Blackburn to Bolton section of the 'Granada Telethon Pullman' on 19 July 1992. This all-day tour of the north-west started from Liverpool and visited Wigan, Southport, Blackpool, Preston, Morecambe, Carnforth, Clitheroe, Blackburn, Bolton, Rochdale and Oldham Mumps, before terminating at Manchester Victoria. Lengthy stops at each station allowed plenty of time to raise money for Granada Television's 'Telethon 92' event.

THE MANCHESTER & LEEDS Railway
was sanctioned by Parliament in 1836 as
a railway commencing at Manchester
and terminating at Normanton, from
where trains would reach Leeds via the
North Midland Railway. Although Leeds
is only 35 miles from Manchester, the hilly
nature of the surrounding terrain meant
that the company engineers adopted
a circuitous route through Rochdale,
Todmorden, Hebden Bridge and the
sinuous and steep-sided Calder Valley. The
'Calder Valley' line was opened between
Manchester and Littleborough on 3 July
1839, and further sections were brought
into use on 5 October 1840 and
3 January 1841. The railway was completed
throughout on 1 March 1841.

The completed railway was heavily
engineered, the Summit Tunnel between
Littleborough and Walsden being the
longest in the world at the time of its
construction. This highly scenic line still
forms part of an important rail link between
Manchester and Leeds, although trains
now travel on a shorter route via Halifax
and Bradford. The eastern half of the route
also forms part of separate Trans-Pennine
route via Todmorden, Burnley and
Blackburn.

AMBERLEY   £16.99

ISBN 978-1-4456-4388-5

9 781445 643885

www.amberley-books.com

DENSIDADES ● **DENSITIES** ■ VIVIENDAS **972** DWELLINGS ■ USOS ● **USES** ■

64,5 % VIVIENDA LIVING	**1,9 %** TRABAJO WORKING	**5 %** COMERCIOS SHOPPING	EQUIPAMIENTOS CIVIC FACILITIES	**28,6 %** HOTEL/APARCAMIENTO HOTEL/PUBLIC PARKING

16.420 m² SUPERFICIE DE PARCELA PLOT AREA	**162.580 m²** SUPERFICIE CONSTRUIDA BUILT UP AREA	**62,4 %** OCUPACIÓN COVERED AREA	**11** EDIFICABILIDAD FLOOR AREA RATIO

592 △/ha **944** ⊖/ha

NASA

1:10.000

Studio Gang Architects studiogang.net

225 North Columbus Drive, Chicago. USA, 2004-2010

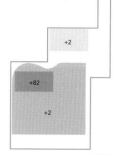

1:5.000

La torre de 82 plantas alberga diferentes usos, que incluyen un hotel, apartamentos, viviendas de lujo, oficinas y aparcamiento público repartidos en 162.580 m² construidos. Históricamente, los rascacielos de Chicago han debido luchar por proporcionar vistas y los nuevos proyectos han de buscar ejes visuales entre los edificios ya existentes. En este sentido, la torre Aqua ha sido especialmente concebida para capturar determinadas vistas muy difíciles de obtener.

Así, los balcones ondulados al exterior de la estructura de la torre proporcionan vistas entre los edificios cercanos. Dichas ondulaciones varían a lo largo de la altura del edificio, dotando al volumen de carácter escultural. La formalización de las terrazas responde a criterios de soleamiento y a las tipologías de vivienda. El resultado es una torre que permite a sus usuarios habitar la fachada del edificio y la ciudad al mismo tiempo.

The mixed-use 82-story tower includes a hotel, apartments, condominiums, parking and offices totaling over 162,580 m². Clusters of high-rise towers in Chicago tell a story of a struggle for views. New towers must negotiate smaller view corridors between already existing buildings. In response to this situation the Aqua Tower is designed to capture particular views that would otherwise be unattainable.

A series of contours defined by outdoor terraces extend away from the face of the structure to provide views between neighbors. These outdoor terraces gradually undulate over the height of the building. Because the shape of the terraces changes from floor to floor, the building presents a sculptural appearance to the city. Shaping of the terraces is further defined and formed by criteria such as solar shading and dwelling type. The result is a high-rise tower that allows residents to inhabit the facade of the building and the city at the same time.

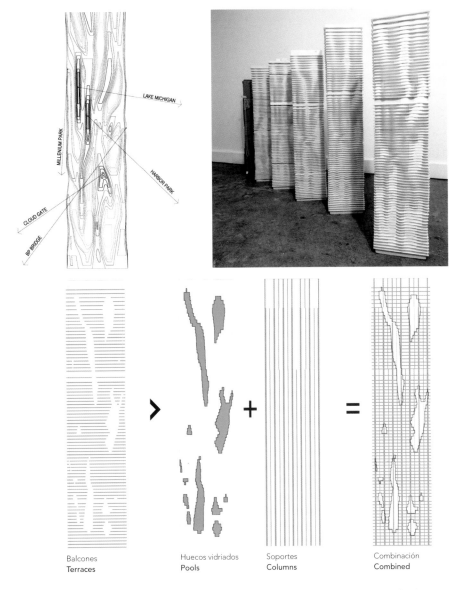

LAKE MICHIGAN

MILLENIUM PARK

HARBOR PARK

CLOUD GATE

BP BRIDGE

Balcones
Terraces

Huecos vidriados
Pools

Soportes
Columns

Combinación
Combined

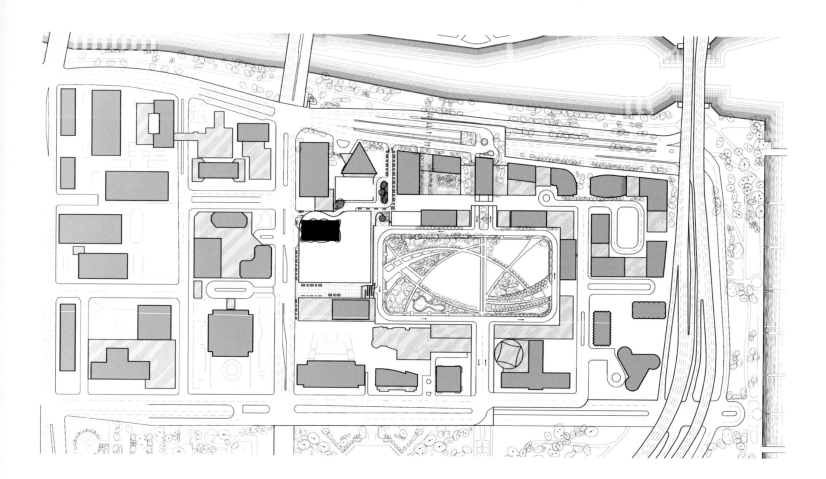

Planta de situación **Proposed maximum building envelope site plan** ◕ 1:5.000

356 Density projects

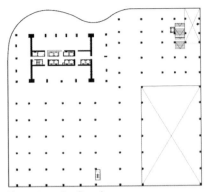

Planta primera **First floor plan**

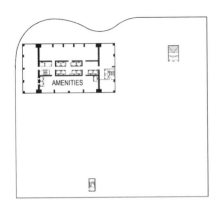

Planta segunda **Second floor plan**

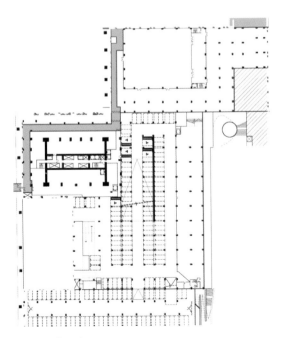

Planta -1 **floor plan**

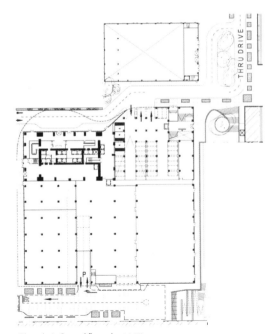

Planta baja **Ground floor plan** 1:2.000

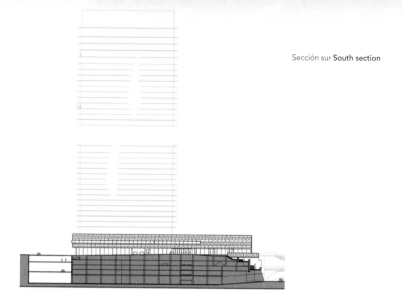

Sección sur **South section**

Sección oeste **West section** 1:2.000

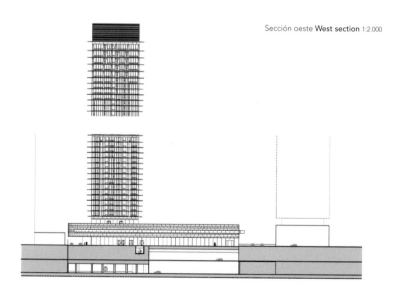

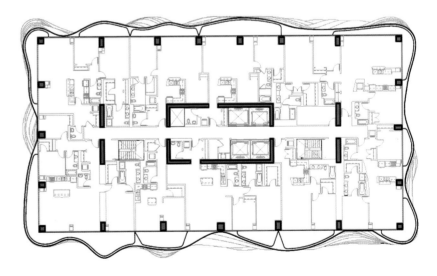

Planta tipo **Type floor plan** 1:500

96,7 %
VIVIENDA   193 🚗
LIVING

TRABAJO
WORKING

3,3 %
COMERCIOS
SHOPPING

EQUIPAMIENTOS
CIVIC FACILITIES

OTROS USOS
OTHER USES

2.081 m²
SUPERFICIE DE PARCELA
PLOT AREA

10.913 m²
SUPERFICIE CONSTRUIDA
BUILT UP AREA

31,8 %
OCUPACIÓN
COVERED AREA

5
EDIFICABILIDAD
FLOOR AREA RATIO

432
⌂/ha

1430
⊙/ha

+19

1:2.500

cnes/spot image, 2007

🔵 1:10.000

NO.MAD Arquitectos nomad.as

Calle Sasikoa, Durango. Spain, 2005-2009

El concepto de vivienda como agrupación de espacios con diferentes necesidades de conexiones y suministros, nos permite realizar una división entre aquellos elementos que precisan de acometidas a la red vertical de instalaciones, elevación o accesos de cada planta, de aquellos que no las necesitan. Dicha dualidad configura una serie de minicadenas funcionales relacionadas con el tamaño de cada vivienda. Podemos enlazar cada una de sus minicadenas y enroscarlas en torno a un núcleo central de comunicaciones.

Entre la cadena de servicios y la fachada, surgen las estancias que se sirven del paisaje y que son variables con la altura. Estos espacios están dotados de una permeabilidad funcional y sensible por las distintas formas de observar y disfrutar del exterior, que se materializan en tipos de aperturas diversos. Aquellas áreas de las fachadas que se relacionan con el paisaje lejano se perforan con espacios-mirador. Las áreas con una percepción visual más próxima se tratan con una piel que permite observar desde el interior sin ser visto. Mediante una disposición ordenada en espiral de los tipos de vivienda con su superficie y cadena de infraestructuras asociada, se obtiene un estado de equilibrio en la organización interna debida a las configuraciones diferentes de las noventa viviendas transformadas por su localización y las incitaciones del paisaje en altura.

The concept of the home as a group of spaces with different needs of connection and provision allows us to divide those elements that require connections to the vertical network of facilities, elevation, or access to each floor from those that do not need them. This duality configures a series of multi-functional systems proportional to the size of each housing unit. We can link each of the multi-functional systems and fix them around a central communications core. Between the services and the facade there are areas that serve as landscape and that are variable with height. These spaces have a permeability that is functional and sensitive because of the different ways of observing and enjoying the outside. These are materialised in different types of openings. Those areas of the facade with a view of the far-off landscape are perforated with windowed balconies. The areas with a nearer visual perception are treated with a skin that allows observation from the inside out without being seen. By means of an orderly spiral disposition of the types of homes with their surface and associated chain of infrastructures, a balance in internal organisation is obtained due to the different configurations of the ninety homes transformed by their location and the incitement of high-rise landscape.

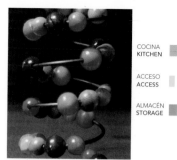

Unidades de servicios **Service units**

COCINA
KITCHEN ▪

ACCESO
ACCESS ▪

ALMACÉN
STORAGE ▪

Tipos de viviendas **Dwelling types**
ESTUDIOS: 0
1 DORMITORIO: 4
2 DORMITORIOS: 38
3 DORMITORIOS: 34
4+ DORMITORIOS: 14
STUDIOS: 0
1 BEDROOM: 4
2 BEDROOMS: 38
3 BEDROOMS: 34
4+ BEDROOMS: 14

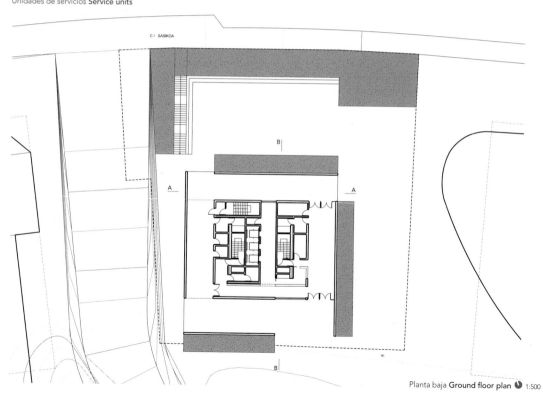

C / SASIKOA

Planta baja **Ground floor plan** 🕐 1:500

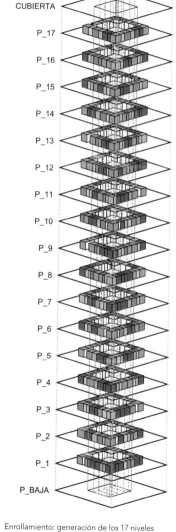

CUBIERTA

P_17

P_16

P_15

P_14

P_13

P_12

P_11

P_10

P_9

P_8

P_7

P_6

P_5

P_4

P_3

P_2

P_1

P_BAJA

Enrollamiento: generación de los 17 niveles
Coiling: generation of 17 levels

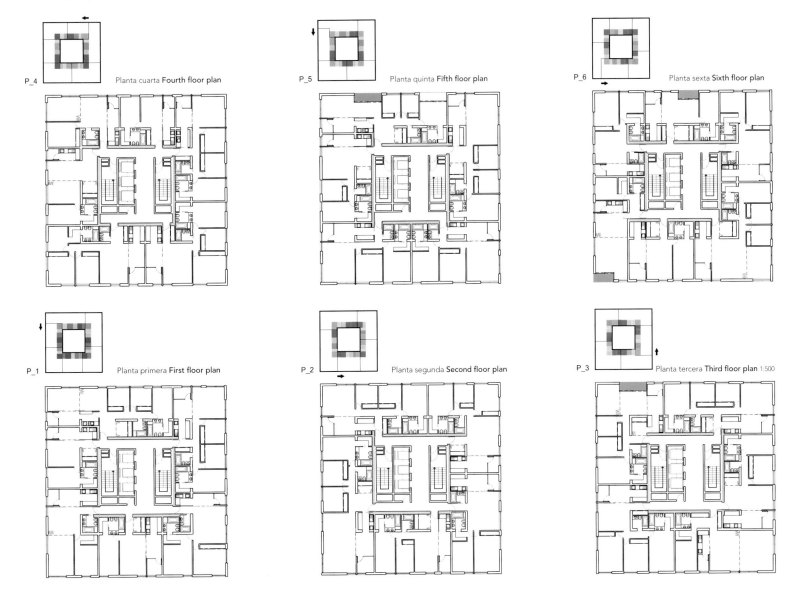

P_4 Planta cuarta **Fourth floor plan**

P_5 Planta quinta **Fifth floor plan**

P_6 Planta sexta **Sixth floor plan**

P_1 Planta primera **First floor plan**

P_2 Planta segunda **Second floor plan**

P_3 Planta tercera **Third floor plan** 1:500

P_13 Planta 13ª **13th floor plan**

P_14 Planta 14ª **14th floor plan**

P_15 Planta 15ª **15th floor plan**

P_7 Planta séptima **Seventh floor plan**

P_8 Planta octava **Eighth floor plan**

P_9 Planta novena **Ninth floor plan**

P_16   Planta 16ª **16th floor plan**

P_17   Planta 17ª **17th floor plan**

Planta bajo cubierta **Under roof plan**

P_10   Planta 10ª **10th floor plan**

P_11   Planta 11ª **11th floor plan**

P_12   Planta 12ª **12th floor plan** 1:500

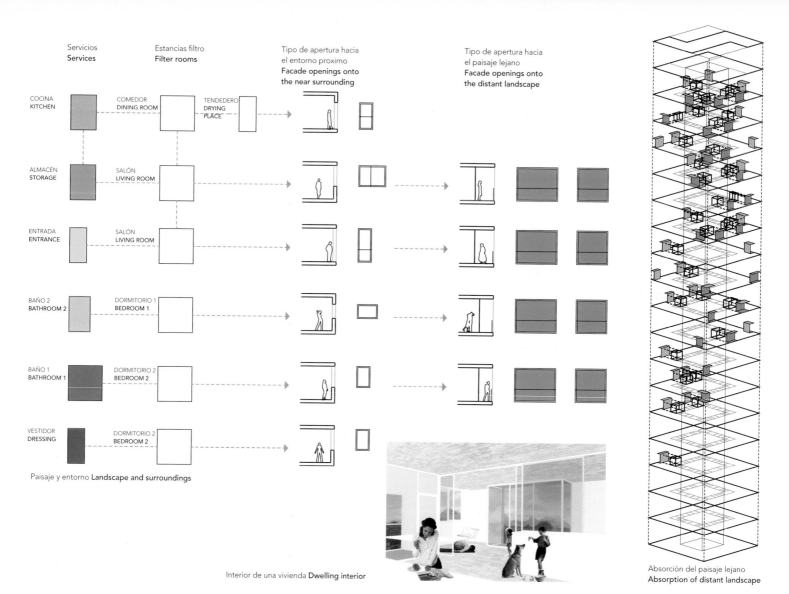

Servicios **Services**	Estancias filtro **Filter rooms**		Tipo de apertura hacia el entorno proximo **Facade openings onto the near surrounding**	Tipo de apertura hacia el paisaje lejano **Facade openings onto the distant landscape**
COCINA KITCHEN	COMEDOR DINING ROOM	TENDEDERO DRYING PLACE		
ALMACÉN STORAGE	SALÓN LIVING ROOM			
ENTRADA ENTRANCE	SALÓN LIVING ROOM			
BAÑO 2 BATHROOM 2	DORMITORIO 1 BEDROOM 1			
BAÑO 1 BATHROOM 1	DORMITORIO 2 BEDROOM 2			
VESTIDOR DRESSING	DORMITORIO 2 BEDROOM 2			

Paisaje y entorno **Landscape and surroundings**

Interior de una vivienda **Dwelling interior**

Absorción del paisaje lejano **Absorption of distant landscape**

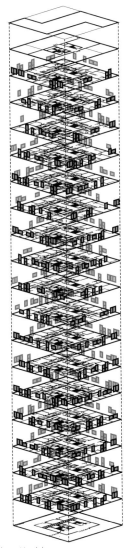

Absorción del entorno cercano
Absorption of near surrounding

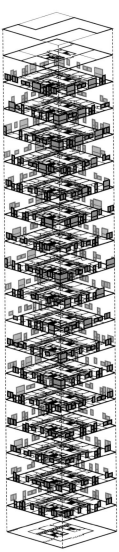

Azar y necesidad
Chance and necessity

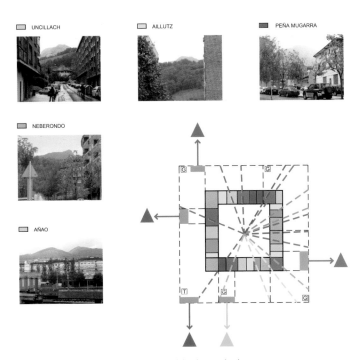

UNCILLACH   AILLUTZ   PEÑA MUGARRA

NEBERONDO

AÑAO

Apropiación del paisaje lejano **Appropiation of the distance landscape**

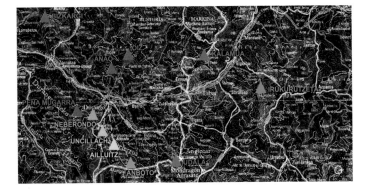

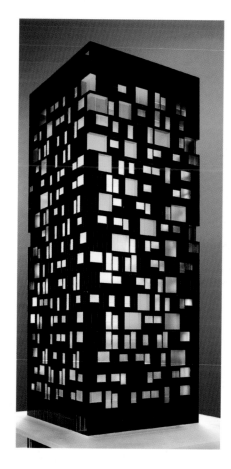

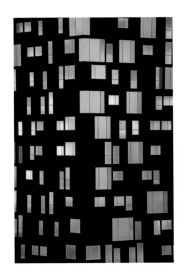
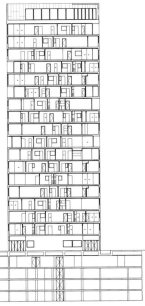

Sección **A Section**

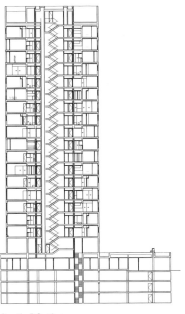

Sección **B Section**

Planta torre **Tower plan**

Generación de fachadas
Facades generation

PAISAJE | LANDSCAPE

ENTORNO | SURROUNDING

Alzado oeste **West elevation**

Alzado norte **North elevation**

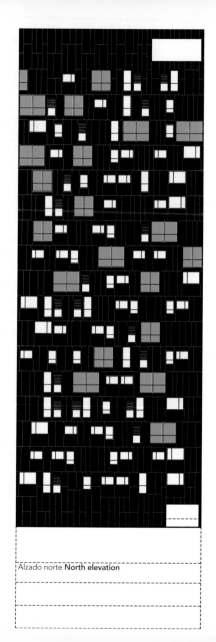

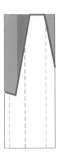

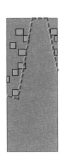

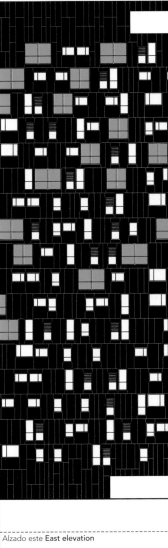

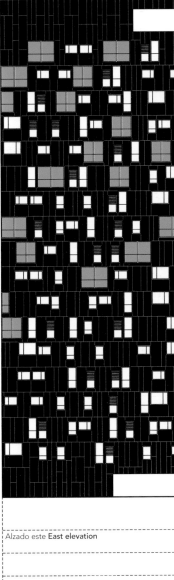

Alzado este **East elevation**

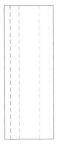

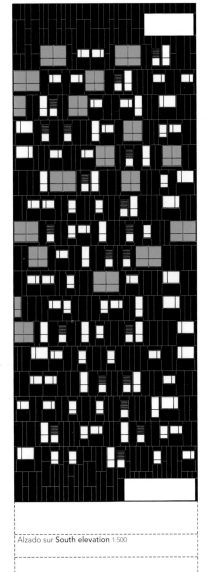

ENTORNO **SURROUNDING** | PAISAJE **LANDSCAPE**

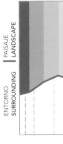

Alzado sur **South elevation** 1:500

DENSIDADES ● **DENSITIES** ■ VIVIENDAS **180** DWELLINGS ■ USOS ● USES ■

662 ⌂/ha   1472 ⊖/ha

75,5 %
VIVIENDA
LIVING

TRABAJO
WORKING

10 %
COMERCIOS
SHOPPING

EQUIPAMIENTOS
CIVIC FACILITIES

14,5 %
HOTEL
HOTEL

2.717 m²
SUPERFICIE DE PARCELA
PLOT AREA

22.239 m²
SUPERFICIE CONSTRUIDA
BUILT UP AREA

35 %
OCUPACIÓN
COVERED AREA

8,1
EDIFICABILIDAD
FLOOR AREA RATIO

digitalglobe, 2007

1:10.000

+26 +33

1:2.500

Rojkind Arquitectos rojkindarquitectos.com

Av. Santa Fe #482, Col. Lomas Santa Fe
Miguel Hidalgo, Distrito Federal. Mexico, 2005-

Ubicado en Santa Fe, al noroeste de la ciudad de México, se plantea un desarrollo de 10 torres de uso principalmente residencial. Cada una ha sido diseñada por un estudio de arquitectos diferente con el fin de obtener las mejores propuestas.
El programa de la torre comprende 180 viviendas de entre 60 y 195 m². El sótano y los primeros 4 niveles están dedicados a espacio público y áreas comerciales, que conectarán las 10 torres. A partir del nivel 28 la torre alberga un hotel de 24 habitaciones con acceso independiente.
Una estructura que actúa a su vez como fachada de estos volúmenes da la rigidez necesaria para poder tener plantas libres al interior, utilizando únicamente como muros de carga la circulación vertical.

Located in Santa Fe, northwest of Mexico City, the development of ten mainly residential towers has been proposed. Each one was designed by a different architectural studio, in order to obtain the best proposals.
The programme of the tower includes 180 homes between 60 and 195 m². The basement and first four floors are dedicated to public space and commercial areas which will connect the ten towers. From the 28th floor, the tower holds a hotel with 24 rooms with an independent entrance.
A structure that also acts as a facade to these volumes gives the necessary rigidity to be able to have open plans on the inside, using only the vertical circulation as load-bearing walls.

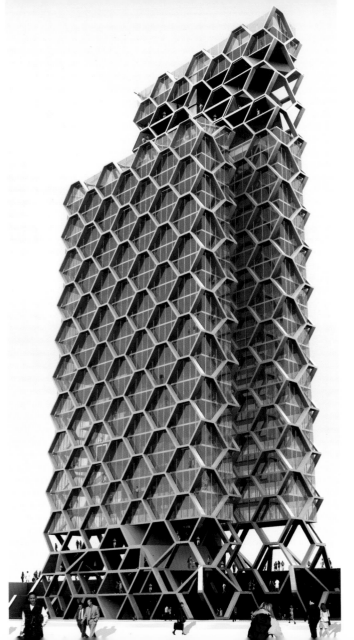

Fachada norte **North facade**

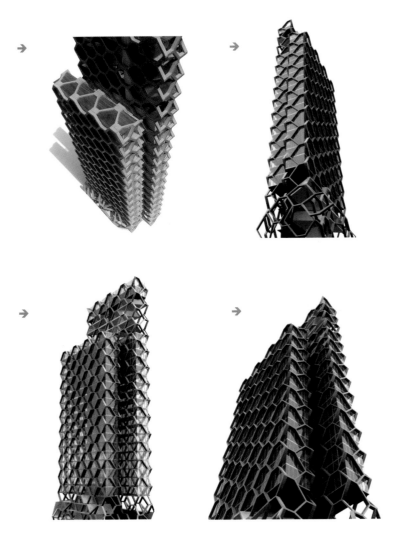

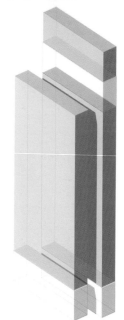

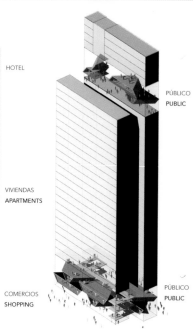

HOTEL

VIVIENDAS
APARTMENTS

COMERCIOS
SHOPPING

PÚBLICO
PUBLIC

PÚBLICO
PUBLIC

Volúmenes **Volumes**

Circulaciones / Usos
Circulation / Uses

Público / Privado
Public / Private

Estructura **Structure**

Tiendas: planta 01-04
Shopping area: floor 01-04

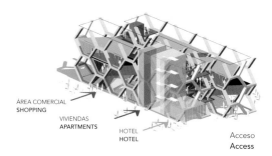

ÁREA COMERCIAL
SHOPPING

VIVIENDAS
APARTMENTS

HOTEL
HOTEL

Acceso
Access

Acceso a la área comercial **Shopping Access**

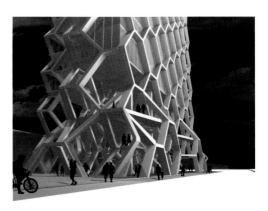

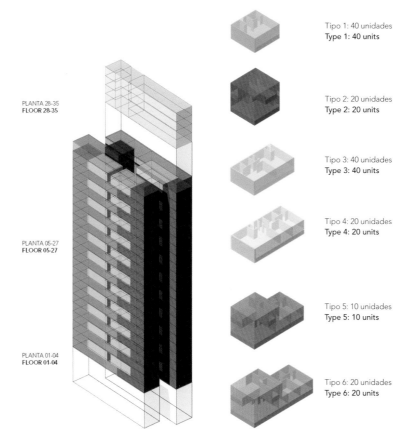

PLANTA 28-35
FLOOR 28-35

PLANTA 05-27
FLOOR 05-27

PLANTA 01-04
FLOOR 01-04

Tipo 1: 40 unidades
Type 1: 40 units

Tipo 2: 20 unidades
Type 2: 20 units

Tipo 3: 40 unidades
Type 3: 40 units

Tipo 4: 20 unidades
Type 4: 20 units

Tipo 5: 10 unidades
Type 5: 10 units

Tipo 6: 20 unidades
Type 6: 20 units

Planta inferior tipo
Typical lower floor plan

Planta superior tipo
Typical upper floor plan

Hotel: plantas 23-35
Hotel rooms: 23-35 floors plan

Piscina: planta 28
Pool: 28 floor plan

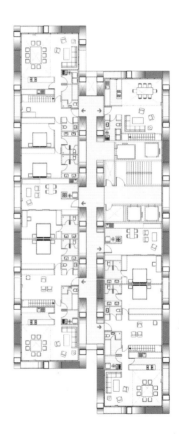

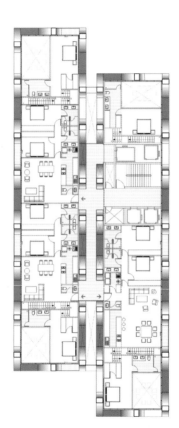

1:500

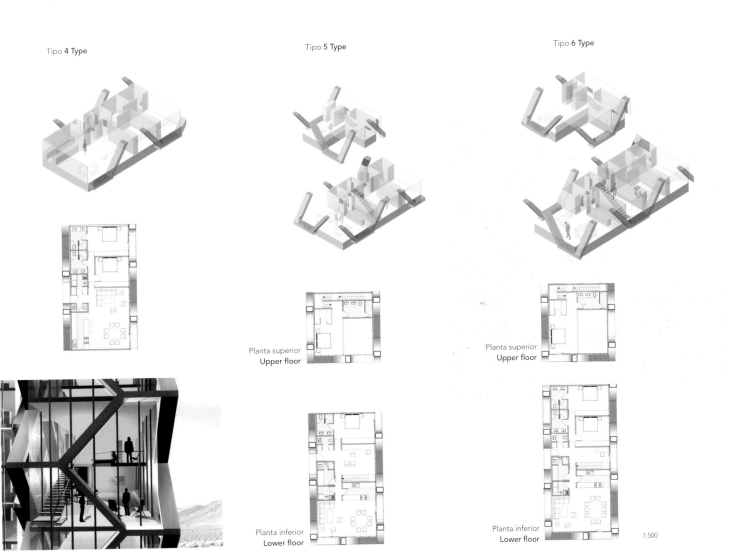

Tipo **4** Type

Tipo **5** Type

Tipo **6** Type

Planta superior
Upper floor

Planta superior
Upper floor

Planta inferior
Lower floor

Planta inferior
Lower floor

1:500

95,5 %
VIVIENDA
LIVING

TRABAJO
WORKING

4,5 %
COMERCIOS
SHOPPING

EQUIPAMIENTOS
CIVIC FACILITIES

OTROS USOS
OTHER USES

1.059 m²
SUPERFICIE DE PARCELA
PLOT AREA

11.656 m²
SUPERFICIE CONSTRUIDA
BUILT UP AREA

73 %
OCUPACIÓN
COVERED AREA

11
EDIFICABILIDAD
FLOOR AREA RATIO

651
△/ha

1511
☺/ha

1:2.500

sanborn/digitalglobe, 2007

1:10.000

Jean Nouvel jeannouvel.fr, beyerblinderbelle.com

100 11ᵗʰ Avenue, New York City. USA, 2006-2008

El proyecto pretende deleitar visualmente tanto a los residentes en el edificio como a los transeúntes en la calle. Su fachada contiene el muro cortina tecnológicamente más avanzado de la ciudad de Nueva York, un mosaico curvo compuesto por casi 1.700 paneles de vidrio de diferente tamaño y colocados con un ángulo específico en cada caso. Este muro cortina enmarca unas vistas espléndidas al tiempo que su textura transcribe la animación, densidad y mutabilidad de Nueva York.

En la base, un paño de vidrio separado 4,5 metros de la fachada del edificio crea un atrio parcialmente cerrado en planta baja, al que asoman jardines suspendidos, los balcones de algunas viviendas y la terraza del restaurante que se encuentra en la planta baja.

Las viviendas comprenden superficies entre 82 y 434 m², y sus acabados se inspiran en las numerosas galerías de arte de la zona.

The project was designed to create visual excitement for both residents inside the building and passers-by on the street. The 23-storey condominium tower will feature the most highly engineered and technologically advanced curtain wall ever constructed in New York City –a curved mosaic of nearly 1,700 different-sized panes of tranparent glass, each set at a unique angle and torque. This curtain wall mosaic will frame splendid views from within the tower while producing an exterior texture that is a poetic analog for the vibrancy, density and changeability of New York.

At 100 11ᵗʰ Avenue's base, a separate sevenstorey street wall of mullioned glass will stand 4.5 meters from the building's facade, creating a semi-enclosed atrium. Within it, suspended gardens of ornamental vegetation and trees will appear to float in mid-air; private indoor and outdoor terraces will extend from residences; and an open-air dining patio for the lobby restaurant. The homes will range in size from 82 m² to 434 m². All of them have super-customized interiors that are inspired by finishings of the West Chelsea district's many art galleries.

Esquema del paisajismo del atrium
Planning sketch for atrium landscaping

Planta primera **First floor plan** 🌣 1:500

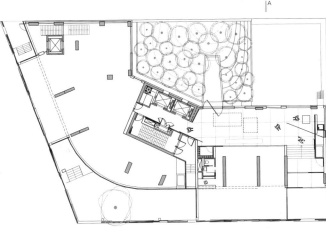

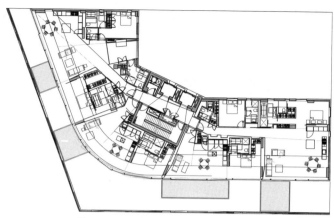

Planta sexta **Sixth floor plan**

Planta quinta **Fifth floor plan** 1:500

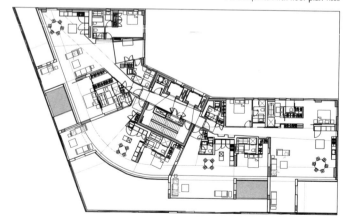

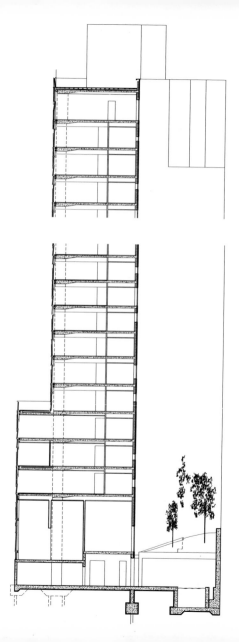

Sección **A Section** 1:500

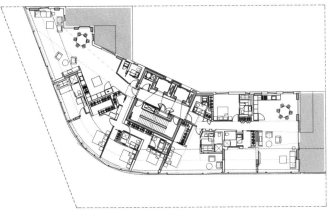

Tipos de viviendas **Dwelling types**

ESTUDIOS: 0
1 DORMITORIO: 32
2 DORMITORIOS: 16
3 DORMITORIOS: 20
4+ DORMITORIOS: 1
STUDIOS: 0
1 BEDROOM: 32
2 BEDROOMS: 16
3 BEDROOMS: 20
4+ BEDROOMS: 1

Planta 7ª-16ª **7th-16th floor plan** 1:500

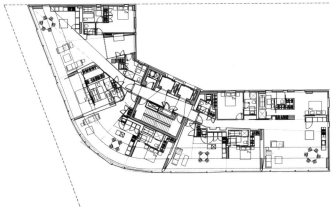

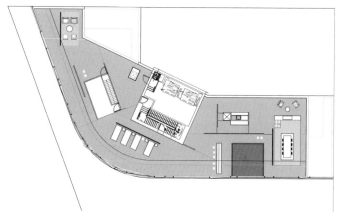

Planta 22ª **22th floor plan**

Planta 21ª **21st floor plan** 1:500

Detalle del muro cortina
Curtain wall detail

97,1 %
VIVIENDA   148 🚗
LIVING

1,6 %
TRABAJO
WORKING

1,3 %
COMERCIOS
SHOPPING

EQUIPAMIENTOS
CIVIC FACILITIES

OTROS USOS
OTHER USES

2.317 m²
SUPERFICIE DE PARCELA
PLOT AREA

23.228 m²
SUPERFICIE CONSTRUIDA
BUILT UP AREA

82,7 %
OCUPACIÓN
COVERED AREA

10
EDIFICABILIDAD
FLOOR AREA RATIO

742
△/ha

1985
◎/ha

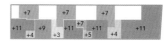

1:2.500

the geoinformation group/interatlas, 2007

1:10.000

X-TU Architects x-tu.com

Promenade des Provinces Françaises, Ilôt 11, Nanterre.
France, 2007-2010

El proyecto responde al programa del concurso, que proponía una fragmentación volumétrica vertical y un perfil urbano variable con volúmenes fragmentados.

En la fachada sur se integran unas grandes aperturas de entre 6 y 10 m que estructuran la organización de la planta y proporcionan transparencia entre las dos calles que delimitan el solar. La fachada sur presenta una fragmentación vertical a escala urbana, y sus volúmenes responden a dos escalas: una primera más grande y monumental y otra menor en relación con la calle de barrio.

En parte baja, los volúmenes están unidos con el fin de consolidar el conjunto arquitectónico.

La unión de los volúmenes horizontales, verticales y transversales forma un paisaje, en cierto modo fragmentado, pero coherente en su diversidad.

El conjunto está pues esculpido en una materia común, y dibuja un perfil urbano recortado sobre el cielo.

This project responds to a competition programme that proposed a vertical volumetric fragmentation that would lead to an urban profile variable to fragmented volumes.

On the south facade there are large six- to ten-metre openings that structure the organisation of the ground plan and provide transparency between the two streets that border the plot. The south facade presents a vertical fragmentation on an urban scale and its volumes respond to two scales, one larger and more monumental scale and another smaller one in relation to the street of the neighbourhood.

In the lower part, the volumes are joined in order to consolidate the architectural whole.

The joining of the horizontal, vertical and transversal volumes forms a somewhat fragmented, yet coherent landscape in its diversity. The whole ensemble is sculpted in a common material and draws an urban silhouette on the background of the sky.

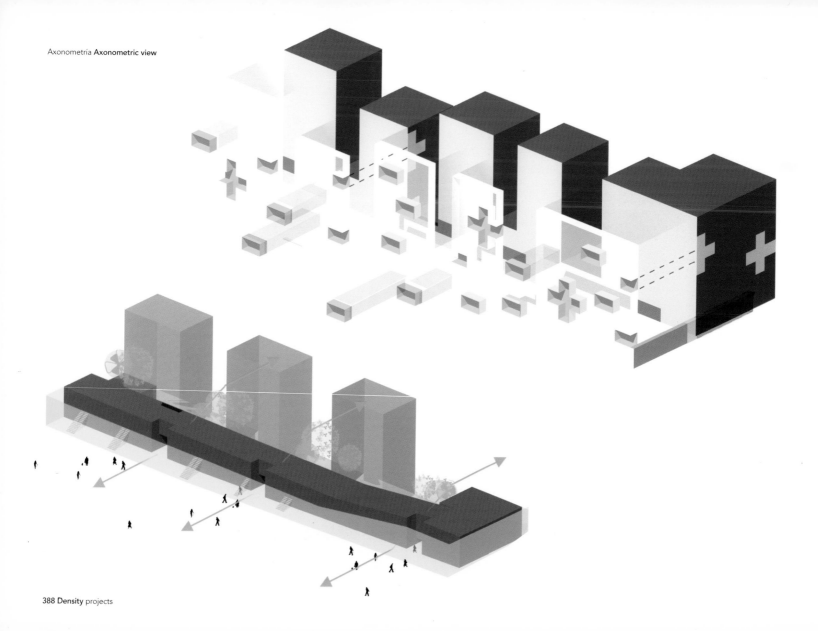

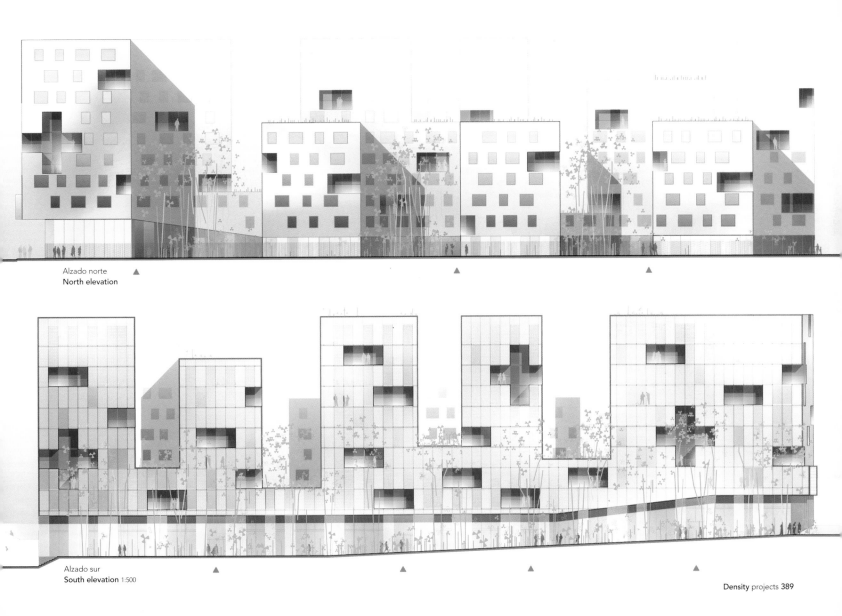

Alzado norte
North elevation

Alzado sur
South elevation 1:500

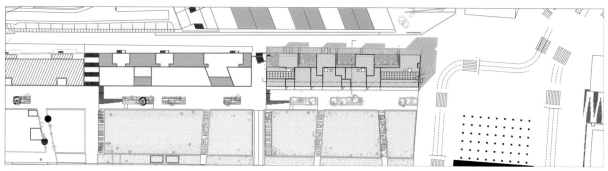

Plano de situación del proyecto de renovación de Promenade des Provinces Françaises
Siteplan of the renewal of Promenade des Provinces Françaises 🌐 1:2.500

Planta baja **Ground floor plan** 1:500

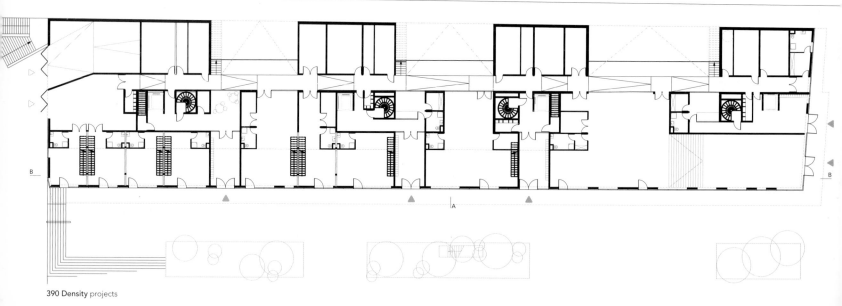

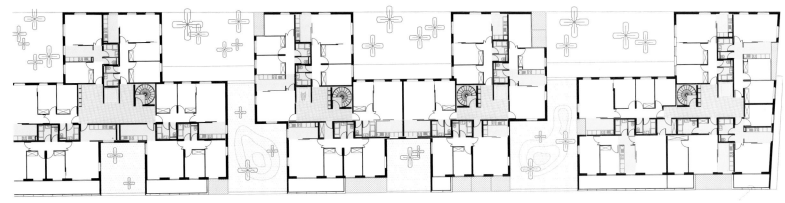

Planta tipo **Type floor plan**

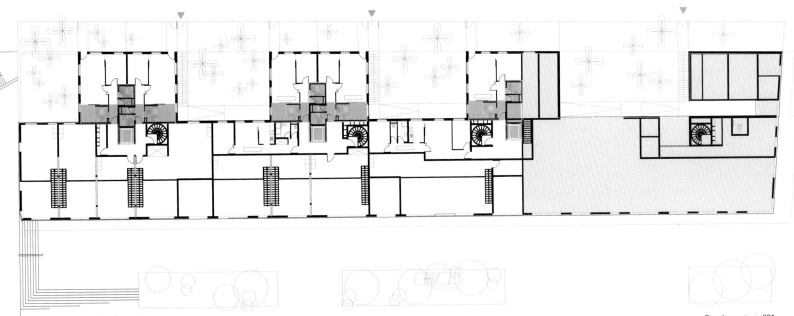

Planta primera **First floor plan** 1:500

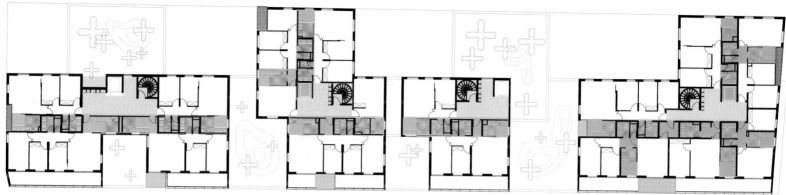

Planta séptima **Seventh floor plan**

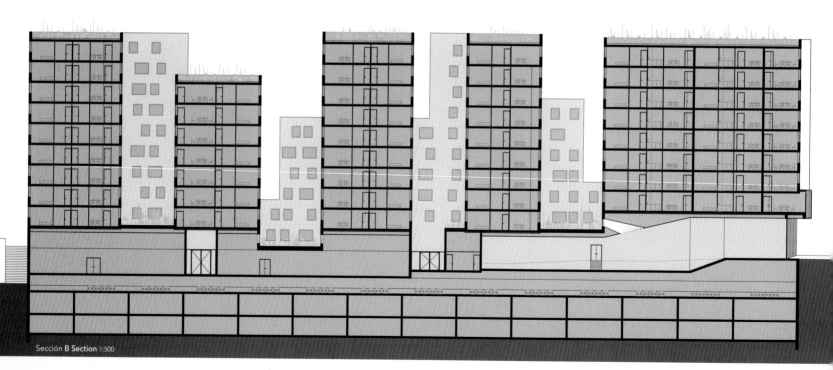

Sección **B Section** 1:500

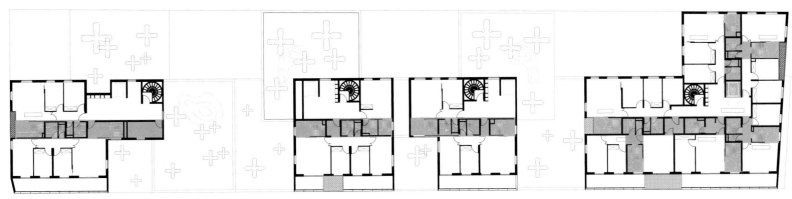

Planta novena **Ninth floor plan**

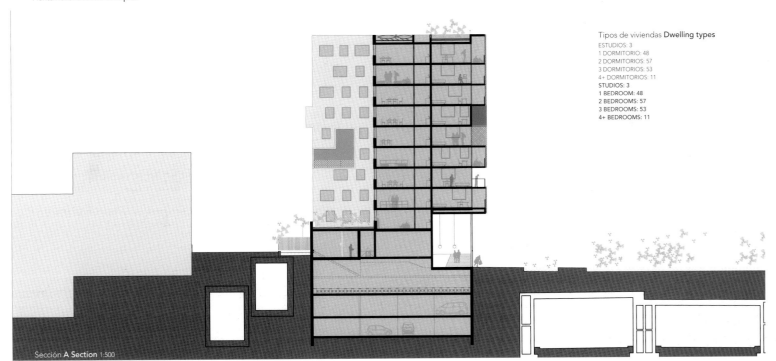

Tipos de viviendas Dwelling types
ESTUDIOS: 3
1 DORMITORIO: 48
2 DORMITORIOS: 57
3 DORMITORIOS: 53
4+ DORMITORIOS: 11
STUDIOS: 3
1 BEDROOM: 48
2 BEDROOMS: 57
3 BEDROOMS: 53
4+ BEDROOMS: 11

Sección **A Section** 1:500

CRÉDITOS **CREDITS**

Eric Lapierre Architecture......08 128-137
Architect: Eric Lapierre
Collaborators in the competition:
Luis Alfaro (project manager),
Bong-Sun Kim, Cyrille Pelliccia,
Giacomo Ortalli, Amélie Evrard,
Guillaume Ramillien, Jedrek Cytawa
Collaborators in the project
developemnt: Sébastien Tison
(project manager), Inbum Kim, Jiyi Yang
Structural engineer: Batiserf
(Philippe Clément et Pierre-Olivier Cayla)
Sustainable development: Louis Choulet,
Stéphane Gautier, Olivier Sudi,
Alain Boudier
Quantity surveyor: Bureau Michel Forgue
(Michel Forgue et Jean-Yves André)
Client: RATP (Logis Transports and SEDP)

Competition, First Prize
Construction documents

Estudio FAM......16 206-209
Architects:
FAM Arquitectura y Urbanismo SLP

Competition, First Prize
Under development

Flexo Arquitectura......27 302-305
Architects: Bartolomé Ramis Frontera,
Bárbara Vich Arrom
Collaborator: Aixa del Rey García

Competition, First Prize
Under study

FÜNDC......05 100-107
Architects: Paz Martin, César Gª Guerra
Project management:
Andries Geerse Stedenbouwkundige

Comission
Under study

Jean Nouvel......35 378-385
Architects: Ateliers Jean Nouvel
Project leader: François Leininger
Executive Architect: Beyer Blinder Belle
Architects & Planners LLP
Landscape Architect: Ateliers Jean
Nouvel with M. Paul Friedberg & Partners
Lighting Design: Ateliers Jean Nouvel
with Whitehouse Lighting Design Group
Construction Manager:
Gotham Construction Company
Structural Consultant:
DeSimone Consulting Engineers
Mechanical/Electrical Consultant:
Atkinson Koven Feinberg Engineers
Curtain Wall Consultants: CCA Facade
Technology, UAD Group, Front
Geotechnical Consultant: Langan
Engineering & Environmental Services
Environmental Consultant:
Roux Associates
LEED Consultant:
YRG Sustainability Consultants
Exterior/Roofing Consultant:
Frank Seta & Associates
Developer/Sponsor: Cape Advisors Inc.
Associate Developer:
Alf Naman Real Estate Advisors
Photos: dbox

Commission
Under construction

Kohn Pedersen Fox......25 290-293
Architect: William Pedersen
Managing Principal: Eugene Kohn
Senior Designer: Trent Tesch
Project Manager: Dominic Dunn
Collaborators: Lauren Schmidt,
Wendy Hanes, Ryan Hayes, Albert Lin
Local architect: SLCE
Mechanical engineer: Flack and Kurtz
Structural engineer: GMS

Commission
Under construction

MAB Arquitectura......02 76-83
Architects: Massimo Basile,
Floriana Marotta

Competition, First Prize
Under construction

**MBM Arquitectes/
MAB Arquitectura**......04 90-99
Architects: Martorell, Bohigas, Mackay,
Gual, Capdevila (MBM arquitectes)
Massimo Basile, Floriana Marotta
(MAB arquitectura)

Competition, First Prize
Preliminary design

MGM Morales, Giles......21 264-271
Architects: José Morales, Sara de Giles
Quantity surveyor:
Francisco Alcoba González
Structure engineering: Insur
Geotechnical engineering:
Cemosa Ingeniería y Control

Client:
Empresa Publica Suelo de Andalucía,
Oficina de rehabilitación de Úbeda

Competition, First Prize
Construction documents

**NO.MAD,
Eduardo Arroyo**......33 360-371
Architects: Eduardo Arroyo
Collaborators: Cristina Hidalgo,
David Rodríguez, Jose Miguel Ortega,
Jose Luis Villanueva, Igor Ortega
Estructural engineering: Joaquín Antuña
Fire consultant: Ingeniería ETXEA
Facade consultant: ABARRE
Exhibition model: Gilberto Ruiz
Client: Gobierno Vasco
Photographer: Federico López

Commission
Under study

**Oppenheim
Architecture+Design**......26 294-301
Architects:
Oppenheim Architecture+Design
Engineers: Ysrael A. Seinuk Engineers

Commission
Under study

Kara Boyd, Yu-Ting Chen,
William Emmick, David Gwinn,
Claire Halpin, Jay Hoffman,
Thorsten Johann, Heather Kilmer,
Phillip Leers, Miriam Neet,
Federico Diaz de Leon Orraca,
Angela Peckham, Sophia Sebti,
Schuyler Smith, Yuki Toyama,
Hannes Wingate
Architect of Record:
Loewenberg Architects LLC
Landscape Architect:
Wolff Landscape Architecture
Structural Engineer:
Magnusson Klemencic Associates
Civil Engineer: IE Consultants
Mechanical Engineer:
Advanced Mechanical Systems
Energy Consultant: Khatib and Associates
Electrical Engineer:
Gurtz Electric Company
Lighting Consultant:
Hugh Lighting Design
Plumbing Engineer: Abbott Industries
Fire Protection Engineer:
McDaniel Fire Systems
Contractor:
James McHugh Construction Company

Commission
Under construction

Tatiana Bilbao/mx.a 13 174-183
Architects: Tatiana Bilbao
Collaborators: Israel Álvarez,
Thorsten Englert, Enrique Salazar,
Guido Ebbert, Carlos Leguizamo

Commission
Construction documents

VMX Architects 14 184-195
Architect: Don Murphy
Project manager: Leon Teunissen
Collaborators: Han Harleman,
Daniel Rivera Pinal, Johan Selbing
Landscape architect: VMX Architects
Structural engineer: Van Rossum
Raadgevende Ingenieur BV
Installations consulting: A. Nieman
Acoustics consulting: Adviesburo Nieman
Interior designer: VMX Architects,
Cristina Ascensao
Client: Pré Wonen/Stichting Sint Jacob

Commission
Construction documents

**Witherford Watson
Mann Architects** 10 144-151
Architects: Witherford Watson Mann Architects
Planning consultants: GVA Grimleys
Cost consultants: John Rowan & Partners
Property and market ad vice: Strettons
Transport consultants: Scott Wilson
Legal Planning consultants: Hammonds
Client: London Development Agency

Commission
Awaiting CPO authorization

X-TU Architects 36 386-393
Architects: Anouk Legendre,
Nicolas Desmazières
Collaborators: Olivier Busson,
Joao Saleiro, Sada Barozova
Engeenering: CET
Ecological engeenering: LESOMMER env.

Competition, First Prize
Under study

a+t

Densityseries